INDEXES
Writing, Editing, Production

by
Virginia S. Thatcher

The Scarecrow Press, Inc.
Lanham, Md., & London

SCARECROW PRESS, INC.

Published in the United States of America
by Scarecrow Press, Inc.
4720 Boston Way, Lanham, Maryland 20706

4 Pleydell Gardens, Folkestone
Kent CT20 2DN, England

British Cataloging in Publication Information Available

Library of Congress Cataloging-in-Publication Data

Thatcher, Virginia Sarah, 1917–
Indexes : writing, editing, production / by Virginia S. Thatcher.
p.   cm.
Includes bibliographical references and index.
1. Indexing.   I. Title.
Z695.9.T45   1995   025.3—dc20   95–5596

ISBN 0–8108–2990–8 (cloth : alk. paper)

Printed in the United States of America

 The paper used in this publication meets the minimum requirements of
American National Standard for Information Sciences—Permanence
of Paper for Printed Library Materials, ANSI Z39.48–1984.

CONTENTS

Preface   v

Introduction   vii

Chapter 1: Methodology   1

Chapter 2: Technique   18

Chapter 3: Format   46

Chapter 4: Alphabetization and Order   55

Chapter 5: Style   89

Chapter 6: Production   99

Chapter 7: Revisions   106

Chapter 8: Specialties   112

Chapter 9: Freelance Indexing   128

Chapter 10: Computer-assisted Indexing   137

Afterword   145

Appendix   150

Bibliography   157

Index   159

About the Author   165

PREFACE

An index may be defined as an alphabetical (or other) number-coded key to information—simply, a listing of terms and page numbers. Yet like many easily defined structures, the simplicity of the definition belies its value. An index is a device essential to a thorough exposition of an author's work.

Other than academic courses on indexing in library science, organized training is remarkable for its absence. In Peterson's *Guide* only one course is listed, and that in the US Department of Agriculture. Otherwise, instruction is largely on the job for staffs preparing nonbook indexes and indexes for encyclopedic reference works. One such is the standard library catalog; in fact, most authorities who have written about indexing are library catalogers. Other examples of nonbook indexes are cumulative indexes (*New York Times Index, Keesing's Contemporary Archives,* and the *Index Medicus*) and legal, financial and business, and science indexes (*Chemical Abstracts*). Such nonbook indexes have little in common with book indexes except for the fundamental purpose of all such devices and the elementary structure. Unlike library catalogs and the various cumulative indexes, for which the patterns for heads, modifications, and cross-references and the terminology preferences are well established, each new book index involves the synthesis of such a pattern from scratch.

Thousands of nonfiction books are published each year in the United States. Indexes for these books are written either by the author—often of one book—or by a freelance indexer. Guidance for such indexing comes from the publisher or from a few sources limited to "recipes" for writing up entry heads and modifications, followed by instructions for filing and preparing copy. Many aspects of the subject are treated inadequately or not at all: a methodology for "thinking" indexing, a survey of the different techniques for preparing an index (not just the author's preference), and the basics of processing an index for production. A thorough treatment of the subject also requires attention to index revisions, indexes for different disciplines, business practices for the freelancer, and computer-assisted indexing. This book proposes a methodology and technique for preparing a quality back-of-book index suited to the subject of the work within the limits imposed by costs and the publishing schedule.

INTRODUCTION

The telephone book as a list of names, alphabetically ordered with a number-coded key to information, satisfies the requirements for an index. As this example suggests, the principle of an index as a pointing device has uses other than for unlocking the contents of a book. Current applications of the index form are library catalogs, cumulative indexes, financial and business indexes, indexes of abstracts in science and technology, and periodical indexes issued annually. Archives of any sort may also be indexed, as may any accumulation of data or things.

Here, however, we are concerned with one specific kind of index: the index to a book. Such an index has characteristics unlike any other. Whereas the index types listed above are on-going publications, reissued periodically, with a fixed format and style, and often produced by a resident staff of indexers, the book index is a one-time performance, with many alternative formats and styles, and often produced by a one-time indexer, an alternative indexer being an independent contractor. The discussion of indexing in the following chapters deals with this distinctive character of the book index and proposes strategies and tactics for solving attendant problems.

The idea of a book index has ancient roots. While indexes were not common until the sixteenth century, several devices were used before that time to indicate what was in a manuscript. Roman authors (for example, Seneca) made an abstract of a manuscript's content; Cicero called such an abstract an ''index.'' Some old manuscripts also carried an alphabetical listing of names, but until the invention of printing, such listings were not in general use. Other terms used for this device were *calendar, catalogue, inventory, register, syllabus,* and most often, *table. Table* was commonly used until the beginning of the seventeenth century. During the nineteenth century, the form of the index became

increasingly functional. Interest in the device led to the organization in Great Britain of the Index Society in 1877; the society
subsequently undertook to promulgate indexing rules. In 1969 the
American Society of Indexers was organized by students at the
Columbia University School of Library Service.

With the introduction of computer-produced indexing and
non-display indexes designed for electronic searching, a need for
simplification of filing rules became apparent, as did a need for
common organizing principles for various keys to information—
from print indexes (back-of-book indexes) to the most complex
technology for information retrieval. The first need was met in
1980 with the publication of revised *ALA Filing Rules* by the
American Library Association. The second need was met in 1993
with publication of proposed *American National Standard Guidelines for Indexes and Related Information Retrieval Devices* by
the National Information Standards Organization. For the most
part these rules and standards have been followed in this book,
adapted where necessary to meet the requirements of specific
markets for back-of-book indexes.

With few exceptions, book indexing has never been regarded as
a skill to be systematically developed. In his preface to *How to
Make an Index* (1902), H. B. Wheatley observed: "It was once a
common opinion that anyone without preparatory knowledge or
experience could make an index. That that opinion is not true is
amply proved, I hope, in the chapter on the 'Bad Indexer' "
(London: E. Stock). The idea that indexing requires no special
skills still has currency today. The reasons are not hard to find. A
compelling one is the belief that the author is the best and, in the
opinion of some, the only person qualified to write the index for
his book.

While it should be admitted that the author knows the content
of the manuscript better than anyone else, it does not follow that
the author is equipped to show off that content in the distinctive
form of an index. This is especially true since for many, if not
most authors, the publication of a book is a one-time experience.

A publisher's perception of indexes and indexing is colored by
practical issues of time and money. Since realistic negotiations
with an author and/or indexer about indexing cannot be made
until the last stage of production—when the overriding drive is to
put the book to bed—the publisher has no reason to view an index

as other than a nuisance. Also, since in one way or another, the author will pay for the indexing, the publisher's answer to the question of "what indexer" is understandably, "the author."

Negotiations for an indexer may take any of several courses. Under the prevailing system, the author may prepare the index him/herself. Again, the author may make arrangements with a professional indexer, but more often the decision is to have the publisher secure an indexer and pay for the work from royalties.

In publisher-indexer negotiations an agreement is reached about fees. Also discussed is a tentative schedule for delivery of page proof and the index manuscript. Occasionally, a publisher will want a house style followed, or an index written to space. Also the author sometimes has exceptional expectations with respect to index content.

DEFINITION OF AN INDEX

In describing what an index is, it is useful to make clear what it is not. An index is not an outline of the contents of a book. The farther away the indexer keeps from the rules of outlining, the more likely it is that a good index will result. What pushes the indexer toward "outlining" is that index entries have modifications and submodifications, much as an outline has subpoints for purposes of development. Unlike an outline, designed to expose the organization of a work, the purpose of an index is to expose the substance of the work.

An index is not a concordance or a list of terms (word list) peculiar to a discipline. Sometimes an author makes up such a list to be used in index preparation; in such a list the relationships essential to an informative index are missing. (An extension of this idea is that an index pattern can be imposed on a text, such as a model from another index; to the contrary the model [or pattern] for an index must be drawn from, and be congenial to, that text.)

An index is not a synopsis (digest) of the text, nor a recapitulation of the table of contents. When an index attempts to duplicate the text in a synopsis, the real message of the text cannot help but be impoverished.

Sometimes an index incorporates a chronology—or a glossary—or a fact summary. Whether the purpose of such devices is satisfied more economically when combined with an index is open to question. In any case, an index designed to be something *more* is likely to be something *less* as an index.

The *form* of an index entry is entirely different from the form of the text, the form of the entry being somewhat like that of a table. The information path on an index is *vertical* (down the page), not *horizontal* (across the page) as is true of text. The entries are arranged in columns, usually two but sometimes three or four to a page. In order to convey a strong communication signal within the limits of restricted space, a minimum of type must be used effectively. This means that devices of limited or forbidden use in ordinary text become functional in an index—abbreviations, figures, symbols, and ellipses, for example.

Preparing copy for index entries is also entirely different from composing prose for text. Prose composition *moves* to unfold the substance of the text. To the contrary, index copy preparation consists of a succession of *stops*. The indexer, in examining the text for indexing material, is not looking for a developing message—a thesis, a theme, or hypothesis. In truth, the indexer's mind set is the same, and at the same time the reverse, of the mind set of an index user. Both are looking for *cues to content:* the index user for cues *to* text substance in the index, the indexer for cues *in* the text substance *for* the index. In this search for cues to substance, the indexer looks not for information (facts) but for cues to that information. In this search the most helpful resource is landmarks that mark the boundaries to a passage, for example, chapter heads, center heads, and side heads. Such landmark heads are excellent raw material (*cue terms*) for index entries. Chapter 1, "Methodology," treats in detail the extraction and manipulation of such cue terms for construction of index entries.

A third difference between text and index is that the index has faults in display of content peculiar to the form. These faults are violations of accuracy, conciseness, and consistency.

Accuracy and precision: The page number code must be not only *right* but *exact*—not *approximate*. When the text matter cued by the entry head (or modification) is to one page only (461), the page number code should not be 460–462, and when the passage extends beyond one page (as 460–462) it should not be coded with only one page.

A cross-reference should be unequivocal; it must use a prede-termined terminology preference. One cross-reference fault is the *blind* cross-reference. For example: TNT. *See* Trinitrotoluene. Where *Trinitrotoluene* should be, there is no entry. Such a cross-reference is called *blind* because there is no entry to *See.* A variation is the "entry chase"—a cross-reference to a cross-reference: TNT. *See* Trinitrotoluene *and* Trinitrotoluene. *See* TNT. (The entry sought is probably *Dynamite.*)

Conciseness: An index entry should *cue* the text message, not try to be that message. An index user turning to an index has in mind a single term (noun, noun phrase); that term is what is wanted in the entry head. No more. And should the user further seek a subclass of that term (a modification), he/she wants only to see the modifying term or phrase. Conciseness in entry copy means not only selection of exact term cues to the text message, but also elimination of useless particles in modifications (con-junctions and prepositions).

Consistency: In planning an index the indexer has choices between format designs and style. *Not* choosing among alterna-tives before work begins results in annoying blemishes: mixtures of line-by-line and paragraphed design; of word-by-word and letter-by-letter alphabetizing; of capitals and lower case for entry heads; and of codes for illustrations, tables, notes, and references. *Indexing is details.* Furthermore, it is just these kinds of faults that mar the message and turn off users and reviewers, including buyers of books for institutions (schools and libraries), with unwelcome consequences for both author and publisher. These faults are a direct result of lack of a methodology. Without a methodology such faults may not become obvious until the index is being assembled, and often not until the work is in type.

From this overview of indexes and indexing, it is possible to extrapolate something about the nature of the work and the successful worker. Indexing is detail, but not insignificant detail, requiring, as it does successively, knowledge, analysis, selection, classification, synthesis, and ultimately creation. Indexing is confining and time-consuming, but most of all challenging. Indexers find considerable enjoyment and satisfaction in their work. The personality traits that favor success for an indexer may be translated into guides for designing an indexing job:

1. Formulation of a work plan and ability to stick to it
2. Orderly arrangement of materials
3. Attention to deadlines without panic, and ability to pace the job accordingly
4. Drive toward job completion; avoidance of getting sidetracked
5. Unremitting attention to detail; the "bricks" and their step-by-step arrangement being as important as the design—perhaps the most important principle.

In trying to achieve quality for back-of-book indexes, what are a publisher's options? There are no criteria (in terms of training and experience) for judging an indexer's competence, and few opportunities for training. While a curriculum vita and a sample index give some indication of what to expect, such evidence is not available for the author-indexer. In fact, the indexer must be judged by the delivered index, and that at a time when the publisher is driving toward a publication deadline. This book is designed to help resolve that dilemma by detailing a process for the would-be indexer.

This book is organized chapter by chapter in a step-by-step approach to the making of an index. These steps are:

1. Projection of a methodology for the text at hand—chapter 1
2. Techniques for manipulation of the text matter to form index entries—chapter 2
3. Projection of a design for the index format—chapter 3
4. Arrangement of entries to meet standards of alphabetization and order—chapter 4
5. Markup of copy to conform to the publisher's style—chapter 5

Subsequent chapters deal with production decisions, index revisions, freelance indexing, and the role of the computer in index preparation.

To maximize the usefulness of this book, each chapter and each section includes *all* the information pertinent to the phase of index preparation being described. As a result some definitions, methods, and techniques are repeated.

Head
Book publishing, xx

Modification
Book publishing, xx
  economics of, xx

Submodification
Book publishing, xx
  economics of, xx
    marketing principles, xx

Inversion
Jackson, Andrew, xx

Cross-reference
Publishing. *See* Book publishing; Periodical
  publishing
Book publishing. *See also* Production

Alphabetizing

Letter by letter	Word by word
Book	Book
Bookbinding	Book louse
Bookkeeper	Book value
Book louse	Bookbinding
Book value	Bookkeeper

Line-by-line pattern
Book publishing, xx
  economics of, xx
  editorial policy, xx
  production factors, xx

Paragraphed pattern
Book publishing, xx; economics of, xx;
  editorial policy, xx; production
  factors, xx

DEFINITION OF TERMS

The terms (with synonyms) used to define the parts and format alternatives for an index are given here for quick reference. Expanded definitions are in the text.

Entry. The unit of an index that points to the concept the searcher is looking for, made up of a head and possibly modifications, submodifications, and cross-references along with page number keys.

Head (heading). A keyword or phrase introducing an entry and determining the alphabetical order.

Keyword (key term). The significant noun (noun phrase) in the head.

Modification (subentry, subhead). A word or phrase that defines a specific aspect of the concept identified by the head.

Submodification (sub-subentry, sub-subhead). A secondary word or phrase that limits the specific aspect of the concept identified in a modification.

Inversion. An alteration in a heading phrase to place the keyword first.

Cross-reference. A pointer from a synonym (or alternative term) to guide the searcher to the head where the concept sought is indexed. The directives are *See* and *See also.*

Letter-by-letter alphabetization. Arrangement of entries by the successive *letters* in the heads.

Word-by-word alphabetization. Arrangement of entries by the order of *whole* words in successive entries.

Line-by-line (entry-a-line, indented) pattern. The entry head and each modification and each submodification begins on a separate line, the exception being an entry head with a single modification.

Paragraphed (run-in, run-on) pattern. Modifications follow the head, the type being run in (run on) line by line.

CHAPTER 1

METHODOLOGY

Methodology decisions for indexing may be summed up as the two goals of index entry preparation: (1) making the ideas in the text available to the researcher, a matter of panning out the significant terms; and (2) assembling these terms in an accurate and orderly pattern, a matter of providing specific pointers to the places in the text where the ideas are to be found by page numbers or another key. How well each of these goals is realized depends on the thoroughness of the indexer's formulation of a methodology.

If an index is conceived of as being a structure, the methodology is the builder's plan, and the indexer is the builder. The importance of a methodology plan cannot be overestimated: without it, the structure (index) will be faulty in design, will not stand up, and will be denigrated by the user. The plan must be intrinsically sound; the design recognizable and consistent; and the building "blocks" solidly constructed and efficiently assembled.

In essence the formulation of a methodology is the process of arriving at basic decisions regarding indexing strategy and tactics: decisions for converting one form of information (the text) into another form (the index entry), the key to the text information. It sets forth the order of tasks: text analysis, entry preparation, alphabetization (and ordering), format (design), and styling, all needed for the indexer to efficiently gather together the many strands of the indexing process.

INFORMATION GATHERING

Several kinds of information are needed for working up a methodology. Some are intangible and have to do with interper-

1

sonal factors—dealing with the people and realities of the publishing business. An indexing project is not only about indexing materials and their manipulation. Rather, author, publisher, and publishing house staff are also involved. An author has egoistic and financial concerns since ultimately his/her reputation is affected by the reception of his book, and one way or another the author pays the indexing bill. The publisher likewise has a reputation and pocketbook to protect as well as an inflexible publishing schedule to keep on track. The publishing house staff, like the publisher, is driven to get the index written in order to bring their work on the book to a close. Nor is the indexer immune to personal concerns about an indexing project, particularly if dependent on the work for a living.

Many indexer-publisher relationships go on for many years with mutual satisfaction. The publisher has recognized standards and provides proof of good quality, delivered on schedule. The deadlines are reasonable, the fee schedule is good, and the payments are on time. The publisher accepts the indexer's prerogatives as a responsible worker and resists micromanaging. Since the opposite of these desirable conditions is also possible, the index methodology must include room for shifting tactics at any stage.

The place of interpersonal factors in information gathering may be illustrated by describing the process from the first contact by phone with a publisher with an indexing project in mind. By the time the phone call is ended, the indexer will (or will not) feel at ease about taking on the job and will also have obtained a number of facts about the project: the subject of the work (discipline represented); author (or authors or members of a symposium); number of pages; kind(s) of index(es) required (subject only or subject supplemented by author, title, first lines, cases, etc.); likely proof delivery schedule; manuscript delivery deadline; fee arrangement; and the possibility that "conditions" may be set by publisher or author. (See following examples.)

With the delivery of first page proof, the methodology begins to take shape. The terminology and depth of coverage of the subject; the organization of heads (chapter, center, and side); and the inclusion of tables, illustrations, notes, and other supplementary material, such as end-of-chapter lists of references, forecast the complexity of the indexing job in terms of mining entry material from the text and also point to an appropriate index format and style.

Another message from the page proof should not be ignored: Upon careful scrutiny, is the proof clean, that is, devoid of typographical errors and discrepancies in spelling (of proper names, for example)? Is all the material promised included in the delivery? Typographical errors and incomplete proof with gaps in continuity signal the need for time-consuming work unrelated to the basic indexing job.

Two examples from experiences with information-gathering for a methodology point out how variable and sometimes challenging the process can be.

EXAMPLE 1—The client firm was a major publisher of scientific books with a stable of well-known authors. The contact was the managing editor, an agreeable fellow, working under considerable pressure, as did the rest of the editorial staff. It was not unusual for this publisher to have a commitment to display the book at a scientific meeting and to set deadlines accordingly. The pay was good. Proof deliveries were usually on schedule.

The book to be indexed had 600 pages. Proof was to be delivered in batches with a manuscript deadline three weeks from the last delivery. It was known from prior experience with the firm that uncorrected proof might be supplied for indexing with errors and inconsistencies in proof and page makeup. Changes in proof were possible after proof delivery. Separate subject and author indexes were requested.

Proof pages for indexing included tables, illustration, notes, and end-of-chapter references. The format used chapter heads, center heads, and side heads. Some pages were misnumbered and several were missing.

Methodology. The complexity of the assignment precludes undertaking additional indexing except for short books. Time management is essential because of the quality of the proof. On the positive side, the good relations with the managing editor make the anticipated difficulties bearable. The format with heads, legends, and captions simplifies the identification of entry concepts. Text material indicates a fair number of entries per page (five or more). The discipline (science) calls for a line-by-line format. Alphabetization will be word-by-word.

An immediate task is to check proof for continuity and missing tables and illustrations in order to get corrections from the publisher. Indexing will begin with the author index; here inconsistencies between text and reference list in spelling and reference numbers are to be expected.

EXAMPLE 2—The publisher was a university press with a small output. The book was a 250-page text on economics. The author was deceased, and his widow was to act as his surrogate, with the intention of supervising the indexing. She would provide a list of "must" entries. The publisher was called upon the recommendation of an economist for whom the indexer had done considerable work. No other indexer was interested in the assignment.

This is an example of a diplomacy dilemma—a conflict between deference to a valuable client and integrity as a worker. Since letting the widow's comments affect indexing decisions was unacceptable, and since she might be charged for an index she did not approve, no fee would be charged if the index was rejected. There was no manuscript delivery deadline. The page proof would be delivered in batches.

Proof pages consisted of straight text without heads, illustrations, or tables. The style was loose and discursive. The proof was clean; the design simple. The editing was professional.

Methodology. The absence of heads means that guides to content must be supplied by improvising substitutes by text analysis. Two to three index items per page should be adequate. A line-by-line format and word-by-word alphabetizing are indicated. The assignment has no priority and will not interfere with other work.

A few practical matters need to be addressed with reference to specific decisions in methodology formulation: (1) negotiating for a realistic deadline; (2) criteria for separate indexes; (3) index items per proof page.

Since the length of the book, the density of the material, and the problems of creating an organized index out of a text that may not be well organized must all be taken into account in projecting a work plan, the indexer needs to make a realistic comparison of the publisher's expectations (and deadlines) with what is possible within the allotted time frame for getting the work done. Negotiating for a realistic delivery schedule early will reduce the possibility of problems later. For example, if a scholarly or scientific book of 300 or 400 pages is delivered to the indexer in batches of about 100 pages, the index copy should be ready for delivery to the publisher within two weeks after the receipt of the last page proof. For a text of 500 to 700 pages, three weeks after receipt of the last page proof would be a realistic delivery date. If page proof is not delivered in batches but all at once, ten days to two weeks should be added to the schedule for delivery. If the book is for the publisher's general trade list, runs less than 400 pages, and has no illustrations, tables, or supplementary material for indexing, the entire text can usually be indexed in ten days to two weeks, three weeks at the outside.

In adapting a methodology to meet the problems of a book with multiple indexes—not only subject, but possibly names, titles, first lines, or cases—the first question is: does the book really require more than one index? For example, a book with more than 300 authors' names probably requires a separate names index. A legal text dealing with cases requires a separate table of cases; a book on law with few references to cases may need no more than a single index including the case references. Much is to be gained by attacking the material for each separate index as a specific task, with the object of absorbing content (terms relating to concepts) while making ''word'' indexes of authors' names, titles of works, first lines, and so on. With this methodology, the subject index entries are prepared last: scanning page proof for a name or a title index serves to familiarize the indexer with the subject concepts and their relationships as no survey specifically for that purpose can. A further advantage in preparing multiple indexes separately is that all the entries for each index (say, of authors) are ready to be alphabetized and prepared as copy; they do not have to be *pulled out* of an uncategorized accumulation—the product of preparing entries for all the multiple indexes as a consolidated operation. (In computer-assisted indexing, multiple indexes can be prepared concurrently.)

The average number of items per page for an index may range from two to three, five to seven, or at the outside five to ten; which average should be the guide depends on whether the publisher has asked for an index of predetermined length. Also to be taken into account is that a repetitious text will result in fewer entry heads and either more page references or more modifications.

"THINKING" INDEXING—ENTRY CONSTRUCTION

The challenge, once information gathering has defined the outline of a methodology, is to extract significant concepts (terms) from the text to be used in creating an index structure: terms and page numbers taken together and arranged in a pattern. It is a problem-solving exercise in which most indexers find considerable job satisfaction.

Clues to significant concepts are provided by a number of text features. A major source is the page typography, the design showing the organization of the text matter. Type style has different weights and faces, and its use to show the divisions and subdivision of the text matter reveals the organization and relative importance of content. These text dividers are the heads: chapter heads, center heads, and side heads. All such heads include terms for important index entries. These typographic features are also related: center heads being subordinate to chapter heads, and side heads being subordinate to center heads. These subordinate relationships carry over in the relationship between the *content* of the *subsumed passages* in terms of entry heads and modifications: center heads are material for modification of chapter heads; side heads are material for modification of center heads.

Equally useful in concept (term) identification are the legends to illustrations and the heads to tables. In a liberally illustrated text, these sources of significant terms may be better than the text. Terms used in legends and table heads may also be preferred, since often illustrations are selected and tables prepared before any manuscript is written. In fact, these are often the basis for text. (Here, however, a caveat is in order. For the sake of ''variety,'' the author may use different terminology in the text and in tables and legends, or may prepare manuscript without referring to the terminology used in illustrative material. If such terminology inconsistencies are few, the indexer may attain conformity by setting up cross-references from the nonstandard to the standard term. If terminology inconsistencies are many, the indexer should consult with the publisher to find out if the desire is to make corrections in the text or if for any reason the author has legitimate preferences.)

A third aid in identifying significant concepts (terms) is the end-of-chapter list of references, often found in textbooks and serious research reports. This source is useful in firming up term selection from the text when there is doubt about term alternatives.

In this way the text is examined not only for significant concepts (terms) but also for relationships between concepts that reveal structure. It should thus be obvious that an index is not *linear*—built word by word, line by line, or page by page—but *structural*—built by recognizing *relationships* between concepts identifying *larger units,* with inclusive page numbers defining the limits of the passage subsumed under the head. By this means relationships are integrated between concepts over the extent of any passage, which may be an entire chapter.

When the text proof is without heads, illustrations, or tables to be used as clues to garner concept relationships for index entry construction, the indexer must improvise. The needed props are supplied by blocking out each chapter into main sections and subsections. The opening sentence to each section should provide clues to the significant concepts (terms). The relationship of a subsection to a main section would be the same as if the chapter were supplied with typographical clues to center heads and side heads.

With the information gathered from methodology formulation well in mind, the indexer is now programmed to select from the text terms that will illuminate through index entry construction the thesis put forward by the author. In the larger view the term selected should (1) evoke an immediate positive response in the reader (and initially in the indexer) by being succinct and forceful; (2) relate to the subject matter of *specific* text pages and indirectly to the subject of the work; (3) should be meat and not merely a garnish; that is, be sufficient in substance to make it worthwhile looking up. In sum it should be a partial answer to the reason the reader goes to the work in the first place. For example, a reader goes to *A Tourist's Guide to Italian Opera* to find out, not about Italian cuisine, hotels, or "good buys," but about towns, opera houses, composers, and opera patrons that participated in the flourishing of Italian opera. If tips on eating, boarding, or shopping are included in such a text, they should be ignored by the indexer. A *term* must be a *signpost* to a passage. A reader misled by a false selection feels the same as a motorist fooled by a misplaced signpost.

This leads us to *categories* of terms to be selected from the text as material for *entry head* construction.

1. A single term (noun or noun phrase) standing alone and expressing one thing; it must be specific—limiting and sufficient by itself.
2. A term of several parts (noun or noun phrase with modifiers) expressing a single compound concept.
3. A term complex of numerous parts (nouns with modifiers) expressing one complex proposition. (The manipulation of such a complex is an important process in entry construction.)

Index entries in a book on houseplants is an example of category 1. The index would be made up mainly (but not exclusively) of plant names standing alone.

Milk bush
Miracle plant
Mosaic plant
Moss
    club
    Irish
Mother-in-law plant

In the second instance, an example would be a cookbook, the subject being foods and their preparation.

Potato
    baked
    boiled
    creamed

In the third instance, an example would be an economics text. Here term complexes in the text become material for index entries *only after* analysis and manipulation, while in the first two instances, terms are selected directly from the text and readily adapted to entry construction. Examples of such term complexes:

Effects of changing prices on output and employment
Identity between marginal cost and competitive supply curve

International goods movement as a substitute for labor
and factor movement

All of these term categories have grammatical components:
noun or noun phrase, and modifiers, which are adjectival con-
structions, with only essential joining terms, prepositions and
conjunctions. As noted, an essential part of speech for entry-head
construction is a noun or noun phrase—a name of something. One
practice that violates this principle is the use of an adjective
standing alone as an entry head. As shown in the following
examples, the fault (corrected) is partly one of format as well as
logic:

Adjective head	*Noun (noun phrase) head*
Military	Military police
police	Military school
school	Military science
science	
Red	
alder	Alder, red
buckeye	Buckeye, red
clover	Clover, red (or Red clover)
dogwood	Dogwood, red

The rationale for honoring rules of grammar in index construction is a subject of dispute among indexers. Even though an index
is made up of parts of speech in a recognizable pattern, an index
is not a grammatical structure; an index is not designed for
parsing. In other words, an index entry is not a disjointed sentence
with "understood" ellipses. The notion that an index should be
made "grammatically" correct and consistent by striving for
conformity in the use of prepositions and conjunctions is ill-
founded. For "user" convenience and comfort, *sparse* in index
construction is *best*.

One other matter needs clarification before turning to tactics for
converting the raw material (in concepts and terms) extracted
from the text into index entries. An early and frustrating concern
of novices to index construction is not so much what to include as
what to leave out. The approach to indexing by the methodology

described here makes the matter irrelevant, by working *down* from a broad perspective rather than *up* from an accumulation of details. In the first instance only the term is selected that supports and enriches the main theme of a section, chapter, and text as a whole. In the second instance, the terms are chosen at random and without purpose; the process is mechanical and devoid of intellectual input.

A major decision about what to omit may be made at the outset. Both broad concepts and details that are extraneous to the subject of the work—background material and anecdotes—do not belong in the index. Oblique references to Italian culinary practices do not merit entries in the index of a book on French cuisine. The same is true of anecdotes about football teams in a book on baseball. Preliminary matter and back matter, with a few exceptions such as end-of-text notes, are not indexed. In addition, the subject of the work—with some definite exceptions—is not usually a legitimate entry head. To use the foregoing as examples: the book on French cuisine would not have an index entry *French cuisine*. But a *baseball* head could be modified with *origin controversy* and *related sports*. Also some entries with *baseball* as a noun modifier—*baseball bat*—would be possible. The exceptions to this general principle are most noticeable in the field of biography: an index entry head for the name of the subject—for example, Wilson, Woodrow—is needed to assemble in one place modifications covering the details of birth, forebears, education, academic career, political offices, death, and works. None of these terms has meaning unattached to a subject. This biography would also undoubtedly have an entry for Edith Bolling Galt Wilson, with relevant modifications on birth, education, and so on. Having *birth* as a head with *Woodrow Wilson* and *Edith Wilson* as modifications would be patently absurd.

As has been demonstrated, what the indexer looks for when exploring the text for entry material is the entry *head,* the noun or noun phrase that illuminates the message of the passage. Index entry construction is largely a matter of arranging these terms (or phrases) so that the *significant* noun or noun phrase leads off—"heads" the entry, with the modifiers following "in line" according to the projected index design. At the same time, (1) the inclusive-page-number code is supplied, and (2) the preferred term is determined, appropriate cross-references being written up for alternatives.

In deciding which terms among alternative synonyms are to be used to identify concepts, authors, as was suggested earlier, are notoriously inconsistent, often showing preference for a term not recognized by their discipline. Editors are just as lax in pointing out terminology inconsistencies to authors. For example, in the biological sciences alternative terms for species, structures, and conditions are not uncommon. In biography and history, names of persons and places differ according to the context of historical period and language. It may be wise for the indexer to make some tentative decisions in order to have a useful terminology classification to go by, with the understanding that, in editing the index, index entry heads may have to be converted to cross-references and vice versa.

For terms in category (1) the *whole* term is the head; standing alone it meets the essential conditions for a head. The following examples illustrate the point:

Person: Jefferson, Thomas (inversion)   Samuel (prophet)
Place: Harpers Ferry   Gettysburg
Event: War of 1812   Holocaust
Object: Chinese porcelain   *cross-reference from* Porcelain, Chinese
Animal: Greyhound   Cocker Spaniel

In the first example, *Thomas Jefferson* is the head, but to bring the surname forward, the elements are *inverted.*

Examples from category (2) illustrate a primary maneuver in entry construction: modification organization. It also shows how tightening copy eliminates nonessential words.

Raw material	*Entries*

1. Payroll taxes and inflation	Payroll taxes
	    inflation and,
	Inflation
	    payroll taxes, and,

2. Applications for Medi-
   care

Medicare
   applications,

3. Disability benefits and re-
   marriage

Marriage
   disability benefits, and
   marital status and,

4. Foreign policy and
   international system

International system,
   foreign policy and,
Foreign policy
   international system and,

5. Soviet bid for oil concessions

USSR
   oil concessions bid,
Oil concessions
   Soviet bid,

6. Endorsement of Eisen-
   hower Doctrine

Eisenhower Doctrine

7. Termination of American
   economic aid

United States
   economic aid from,
Economic aid
   from United States,

8. Origin of choroid plexus

Choroid plexus
   origin,

9. Hypervitaminosis A of
   infant

Infant
   hypervitaminosis A of,
Vitamin A
   hypervitaminosis of infant,
Hypervitaminosis A
   of infant,

In examples (1), (4), (5), (7), and (9), we have instances of valid *mirror entries:* The head becomes a modification, and the modification becomes a head. Example (9) also demonstrates the possibility of significant *hidden* head material.

What has been shown here is a process of *isolation and recombination: Isolation* of a concept from the text, then *isolation* of its structural parts, and then their *recombination* into index entries. These are the fundamentals of the process of "thinking" indexing, a unique mental process that is in essence a matter of analysis and then synthesis. This process is more dramatically demonstrated in examples of term category (3).

Concept identification:
French Canadian classical revival style in church architecture

Component analysis:
Canada, French Canada, classical revival style, church architecture, architectural style

Concept isolation and recombination

Canada
    church architecture
French Canadian culture
    church architecture
Classical revival style
    church architecture
Church architecture
    classical revival style
Architectural style
    classical revival
Architecture. *See also* Church architecture

With this method many of the faults of a "poor" index are avoided. The concept has not been outlined, as it would be in the following construction:

Canada
    French Canada
        church architecture
            classical revival style

Here, in contrast to the foregoing breakdown, the indexer has forgotten the user of the index, whose need may not be repre-

14 Indexes: Writing, Editing, Production

sented by the word *Canada* but by one of the other terms isolated by component analysis.

In the following simple example of the "thinking" process, the raw material from section head, side heads, and sub-side heads is isolated and recombined and then arranged in an index pattern:

Center head:	Silver and Its Compounds
Side head:	Silver extraction
Sub-side head:	Cyanide process
	Parkes process
Side head:	Silver properties
	Silver uses
Entries:	Silver, 521–524
	Silver
	compounds, 522–524
	Silver
	extraction, 521
	Silver
	extraction
	cyanide process, 521
	Silver
	extraction
	Parkes process, 521–522
	Silver
	properties, 522
	Silver
	uses, 522–524
Index pattern:	Silver, 521–524
	compounds, 522–524
	extraction, 521
	cyanide process, 521
	Parkes process, 521–522
	properties, 522
	uses, 522–524

For *topic indexing* of a scientific periodical, a special technique for identifying concepts is useful. The organization of a scientific report is fixed: title, synopsis-abstract, materials and methods, results, discussion, summary. The title is the most important clue to concept identification and hence index entry content. For a topic index, each ingredient in the title as related to the other ingredients requires an entry. For example, the following entries would be structured from the title *Comparison of glucose metabolism in adipocytes from Pima Indians and Caucasians:*

> Glucose metabolism, in adipocytes, comparison of Pima Indians and Caucasians
> Adipocytes, glucose metabolism, comparison of Pima Indians and Caucasians
> Pima Indians, glucose metabolism in adipocytes, comparison with Caucasians
> Caucasians, glucose metabolism in adipocytes, comparison with Pima Indians

These entries point to the main facets of the topic and their *interrelationships,* the essence of topic indexing. Entries on individual concepts (terms) are insufficient. Next, the exposition in the *abstract* should be compared with the entries prepared from the title; different terms may be used, and there may be amplification of concepts in the title. The topics in *methods and materials, results,* and *discussion* should be compared (extracted) in the same way. From this collection of topic concepts, the topical entries showing the interrelationships are refined. Supplementary entries may be needed when the contribution is to a subject not identified in the title entries. For example, the concept *unifying* the topics of the foregoing title is *obesity.* Hence:

> Obesity, in Pima Indians and Caucasians, glucose metabolism in adipocytes comparison

The same technique may be used for a topic index for any periodical, symposium, or collection of essays having the characteristics of expanded titles and a formal structure identifying facets of the topic.

SUMMARY

An index methodology is the blueprint for its construction by the assembling of materials (prefabricated parts) into a projected design. Information gathering for a methodology begins with a phone call from a publisher making an offer of an indexing job. At the end of the conversation the indexer should know the subject of the book, its length, schedule for page-proof delivery, preliminary deadline for manuscript delivery, and method of payment.

The first batch of page proof deserves careful study to project the framework of the index design: discipline represented; depth of coverage; inclusion of illustrations, tables, and lists of references; use of heads (chapter heads, center heads, and side heads)—all will ultimately determine index format and style and tactics for entry construction.

For index entry construction, the richest source of cues to significant concepts (terms) is the text dividers (chapter heads, center heads, and side heads). Nor only do they supply significant terms but they also, in defining the boundaries of passages, supply the needed page-number keys. (In the absence of such guides, they may be improvised by supplying substitutes by analysis of the organization of sections and then paragraphs in the text.)

The terms selected should (1) evoke an immediate positive response in the reader (and initially in the indexer) by being succinct and forceful; (2) relate to the subject matter of specific text pages and indirectly to the subject of the work; and (3) be sufficient in substance to make it worth while looking up.

These terms also fall into categories with respect to their components:

1. A single term (noun or noun phrase) standing alone; it must be specific and sufficient in itself.

2. A term of several parts (noun or noun phrase with modifier), expressing a single compound concept.

3. A term complex of numerous parts (nouns with modifiers) expressing a complex proposition. Although all of these term categories have grammatical components, an index is not a grammatical structure, and no attempt should be made to make it grammatically correct.

Index entry construction is largely a matter of arranging the words or phrases making up concepts so that the *significant* noun or noun phrase "heads" the entry, with modifiers following. An inclusive page-number code is added; preferred terminology is verified; and appropriate cross-references are written up as needed.

This process of entry construction is one of isolation of concept from the text, isolation of its components, and then their recombination into index entries. These are the essentials of "thinking" indexing, a unique mental process that is, in essence, a matter of analysis and then synthesis.

A special technique for topic indexing is useful for scientific periodicals. Each ingredient of the report title (topic) is significant, not only as of itself, but also in relation to all the other ingredients in the title. As each ingredient is isolated, it is also recombined with all the other ingredients in a series of entries. These entries point to the main facets of the topic and their relationship with all the other facets.

With considerations of time and cost effectiveness of major importance in the preparation of an index, a sense of security comes from knowing exactly what is to be done and how it is to be done. The instrument of this security is a methodology, a plan that lays out a specific strategy and series of tactics for getting the job done.

CHAPTER 2

TECHNIQUE

No one technique is suitable for every back-of-book index. The question is: will the technique produce an index that suits the book, satisfies the publisher, and meets the personal and monetary goals of the indexer. For the self-employed indexer, the technique must be cost effective. Outlay for equipment and supplies and expenditures of time when compared with gross income should leave a net profit sufficient to meet the income needs of the indexer. This means frugality in the selection and management of materials and equipment, and efficient organization of the job. For example, the volume of work and fee scale may make investment in hardware and software and ancillary supplies for computer-assisted indexing unprofitable (See chapter 10.) However, regardless of the technique chosen, the fundamentals are the same for indexing with cards, strips, or a computer.

This chapter proposes alternative techniques for meeting different index requirements, the main variables being subject matter, number of indexes, number of volumes to be indexed, condition of text to be indexed, and production deadlines and space limitations. While entry preparation is the main thrust, technique is also concerned with materials organization, editing and styling, and manuscript preparation.

An analysis of the technical procedure of indexing shows it to be a step-by-step progression whereby single pieces are made, tested, and finally assembled in a meaningful whole.

Indexing technique calls for operations in concert. Separate but related acts comprising one maneuver are completely finished before another is begun. For example, in the major maneuver of entry construction, single acts are: (1) concept identification, term isolation and combination or recombination; (2) terminology confirmation; (3) cross-reference construction, if needed;

(4) entry copy preparation; (5) term inversion and modification construction as needed; (6) copy check for accuracy, that is, spelling, capitalization, punctuation, and page numbers.

The importance of this maneuver cannot be overemphasized. The skill with which it is performed makes all the difference in the ease or distress with which succeeding maneuvers are carried out: alphabetization, editing and styling, manuscript preparation, and manuscript checking.

Lapses in technical proficiency here also account for those errors that are peculiar to indexing, the kind of error that makes a bad impression on, and alienates, users and reviewers. Moreover, there is no way an indexer can be sure that error from technical faults at this stage will be found later on in the collating and editing processes.

MATERIALS

Materials organization for its own sake is meaningless. However, with materials in order, the indexer knows precisely what has been done and what still needs to be done. Regardless of the technique used for entry preparation, continuity should be maintained in the housing of materials. By this means it is a simple matter to recheck a specific text passage and entries prepared from it.

The text for indexing may be in the form of galley proof, page proof, or photostats of page paste-up. It may also be partial or total. So far as materials handling is concerned, the most desirable indexing material is a complete set of final page proof with all illustrations (including legends) and tables in place. While it is true that the time squeeze for index preparation—rarely more than a month with delivery of a complete set of pages and three weeks after the last delivery of proof in batches—makes proof in batches the preferred delivery system, the best situation is that with all pages at hand: the indexer does not have to speculate about the content of chapters still to come. The main problem is that the latest revision—which may or may not be the *last*—is not provided for indexing; the indexer needs to know the likelihood of additional changes to avoid doing work that will have to be redone. A similar caveat applies to accepting without question *any* text material for indexing that is not final page proof. Upon receipt of proof, both the completeness and continuity should be checked; the proofs may be numbered consecutively but not have a logical continuity. If proof is delivered in batches, note should be made of what has been received and when, particularly if there is a commitment to meet a deadline. A noticeable gap in the proof may mean that something has been misplaced, either in the publishing house or in the mail. Putting off inventorying indexing material may bring entry preparation to an abrupt halt when proof or sections of text are found to be missing. Material most often missing is that for illustration: illustrations themselves, legends, tables, and so on. If such material is to be indexed, the publisher should be asked to forward it promptly.

An indexer cannot expect to have the space and equipment that would be ideal for materials organization. Working with galley proof is often awkward, as is handling page proof "two up." A flat top desk is often not large enough. Better space is provided by a kitchen or library table. Cartons for storage of proof (finished, in process, and still to be processed) and index files will reduce the clutter. Such materials organization is vital when an indexer is working on more than one index and must keep the materials separate.

TECHNIQUE ALTERNATIVES

The choice of a technique depends not only upon the kind(s) of index but also upon orientation. An indexer trained as a librarian is likely to approach the job differently from one trained in a publishing house. The librarian, with cataloging experience, is likely to prefer indexing on cards. In the publishing house, where the shortest route from copy to composition is often the order of the day, the preferred technique may be to go directly into composition from cards or a paste-up of copy on slips.

Some techniques that on the surface appear to be slick and easy do not save time or produce the desired result. A technique that tries to bypass the detailed repetitive task of preparing entries *one by one* is only substituting a later agony (in the final alphabetizing, checking, assembling, and editing) for an immediate one. Also, any technique that does not provide for altering or moving single entries or blocks of entries (without new copy preparation) seriously impairs control of the job.

The essential materials for any indexing job are simple: typewriter, paper, cards, pen or pencil boxes; and a miscellany of paper clips, rubber bands, and so on. Use of a word processor to prepare electronic manuscript calls for additional supplies. Accurate typing of original entries goes a long way toward reducing error, which is often difficult to find later in assembling the index.

Indexing with cards. Aside from cards being a "cataloger's choice" for indexing, there are instances where indexing on cards has advantages. Indexing with cards may be the method of choice for a large or multi-volume work or an index that is periodically revised. (Certain types of indexes also may be suitable for revision from electronic manuscript.)

The preference for cards is supported by the fact that cards may go directly into composition, the need to prepare manuscript copy thereby being eliminated. On the other hand, their use is uneconomic unless they are to be used for a revision. Also, composition from cards is at premium rates. Indexing on cards also lacks certain efficiency factors: the visibility of entry copy for checking, alphabetizing, editing, and copy preparation is superior with entries worked up on sheets (strips).

Indexing with strips. Perforated strips or sheets (which may be gummed on the back for paste-up) are less expensive than cards and have a number of advantages. (A substitute is the back side of page proof for typing up the first copy.) After entries are typed up and checked, the strips are separated (or the sheets cut up) for alphabetization. If the copy is "good," manuscript may be prepared by sticking the gummed sections onto manuscript paper and making a copyprint for composition. (The strips from ungummed sheets may be pasted up with rubber cement for the same purpose.) Aside from the cheapness of the material, this gummed strip or sheet technique has visibility advantages that no other technique has. By spreading out the copy sheets already prepared, one can get an excellent overview of what has been done the many times a recheck is needed during entry preparation.

Prearranged alphabetical guide. An alphabetically arranged notebook—or some alternative, such as alphabetized sheets on a clipboard—for alphabetizing index entries as they are prepared may have appeal as a way of avoiding the detail of building an index step by step. An index put together in this way cannot have the solid infrastructure of term and concept relationships that is the mark of a quality index. (See also chapter 10, "Computer-assisted Indexing.")

ENTRY PREPARATION

Index entry construction requires responding to a visual message in the text, translating that message into an information signal, and checking the validity and accuracy of that information signal: briefly, a rhythm of seeing-doing-seeing. Technique development requires, first, learning to *see immediately* the keywords in the *text passage* (not just paragraph or page) being indexed. The second skill is learning to *see and accurately record* page numbers. The third skill is to choose the appropriate term from among alternatives for recording the information in the passage being indexed. Which term should be the entry head and which a cross-reference? What is a needed inversion, and is a cross-reference required? When is identification needed for identical terms? Seeing the *passage* to be indexed in terms of coverage will define areas of emphasis for illustrations and tables as well as text.

Marking proof. Marking proof for indexing (see Figure 1) has two purposes: (1) to guide the indexer (and typist) in entry composition, and (2) to provide a basis for checking index entry copy. Detailed proof marking should show: (1) what should make up the key term, (2) what should be a modification or submodification, (3) which key terms should be inverted, and (4) what should be a cross-reference. It should be mentioned, however, that the seasoned indexer only needs a minimum of proof marking, the purpose being to *guide the eyes* to significant words. For the inexperienced indexer, *detailed* marking of the *entire* proof *before* writing up entries is not necessarily expedient. It is better to mark the proof for the *passage* being indexed (and so record the decision for reference when a similar situation arises) and then prepare copy for the entries in that passage.

When a typist is to record the entries, the proof marking should not only make clear the content of heads, modifications, submodifications, inversions, and cross-references but also show the *extent of the passage* (with inclusive page numbers) when the passage extends beyond the page at hand. Also, "created" entries and cross-references should be clearly written out in the proof margins. The code for marking proof may be improvised by the indexer. One that works is as follows:

For entry head—underline once
For modification—underline twice
For submodification—underline three times
For inversion—underline head once and mark for transposition
For cross-reference—place x under key word; write complete
    cross-reference in margin

In practice it will be found that precise information for the typist in the margins will ensure accuracy and save time.

Most printing crafts workers (union or nonunion) learn their trades through established apprenticeships programs. A substantial number of people, however, learn these trades by working as helpers or through a combination of work experience and schooling.

Most printing unions, in conjunction with ←Printing unions. *See* Unions
management, have established guidelines for apprenticeship programs for the various printing crafts. Many nonunion printing firms have established apprenticeship programs with the help of local printing associations and the employer organization Printing Industries of America. Apprentices often are chosen from among people already employed in various unskilled jobs in printing plants.

The marked proof would be translated by the typist into the following entries:

Printing crafts
    apprenticeships, xx
        union or nonunion, xx
Printing firms, nonunion, xx
Printing unions. *See* Unions

Figure 1

Text overview. A survey of the entire text—or as much as is available from proof delivered in batches—is an essential preliminary to projecting a general index arrangement and defining tentative boundaries. (See chapter 1, "Methodology.") Particular attention should be paid to the table of contents, heads and subheads (for arrangement of both general and specific concepts), legends to illustrations, heads for tables, and the titles and subdivisions of supplementary material, such as appendices. As the text is scanned, the eye should arrest on noun phrases that provide the basic terminology for the subject matter.

In projecting a general index arrangement, the indexer needs to keep in mind the possibility of change as entries are being written up; appropriate alternatives to the chosen arrangement should not be closed out.

Entry formulation. An index is not built page by page but by sections, subsections, and ultimately passages. The subject of the text itself, it will be recalled, is not a legitimate entry title, *with definite exceptions.* In some texts the author may give an overview of the subject in the introduction and early chapters and may also use the terminology of the subject in chapter titles. For example, the introductory material in a college text on economics would probably treat definitions, economic analysis, schools of economic theory, the study of the subject, and so on. Here an entry head would be needed to cover these aspects of the subject:

Economics
    analysis
    definitions
    schools of
    study of

Chapter titles always contain matter for major entry heads, as do chapter sections as identified by heads. To use the example of an economics text, the head to a chapter on *business cycles* would require a major entry head, as would the sections of that chapter on *prosperity* and *depression.* Subsections under the sections could be both entry heads and modifications, depending on their significance and extent of coverage. For example, a discussion of *income factor* in the section on *prosperity* could be treated as:

Prosperity
    income factor
        and
Income factor
    in prosperity

The broad perspective used for formulating entry titles applies to the gathering of the corresponding page number keys. The *extent of coverage* for each entry subject (or modification) should be recorded as *inclusive* pages, not just the page where the passage begins.

This technique of indexing passages and grasping the extent of coverage of a concept (or its modification) in terms of inclusive pages effectively divides the text into manageable areas for working over. In other words, once the limits of major sections of the text are identified, the discussion within each section may be examined for pertinent entry heads or modifications.

The appropriate *key terms* are identified by analysis of linked concepts, followed by isolation of concept components, and then the recombination of these components into new formulations.

The facile conversion of text matter into index entries depends on attention to certain terminology criteria. During text analysis the terminology is manipulated to obviate problems in pulling an index together. These criteria for terminology preferences are:

1. Singular vs. plural form
2. Short vs. long form
3. Positive vs. negative form
4. Noun vs. adjective form
5. Noun phrase vs. noun modified by adjective

Entry copy preparation. As will be emphasized throughout this manual, each step toward a finished index should be taken with care; stumbles lead to defects in the final product. Copy must be prepared for *every key term and modification.*

The publisher's format preference should be reviewed before copy preparation: the basic pattern, whether line by line, paragraphed, or some combination; and the style for entry heads, whether capitals or lower case; for cross-references; for page number keys, whether or not inclusive; and for keys to illustrations and tables. (See also chapter 5, ''Style.'') Rechecking should catch inadvertent error on the spot; particular care should be taken in rechecking page numbers.

If the index is being prepared on cards that are to be used for composition copy, entries should be typed up as if the card copy were to be final after editing. The same holds true if slips are to be assembled as copy for composition; only essential editing should ''dirty'' copy prepared by this one-stage technique.

Illustration and table entry copy preparation. Illustrative material is usually related to the text; the illustration (or table) is described in the text and referred to by *figure* or *table.* The appropriate page key for the index entry is expanded to identify the illustration (or table); indexing such illustrative material is integrated with indexing the text: the key terms for the illustrations are the same as those for the text. (It will be recalled that illustrations and tables are important clues to key index terms, for which correspondence is sought in the text.)

Illustrative material related to the text may precede that text, be included within the compass of the text passage, or follow the text. The *specific* location of the illustrative material must be identified in the page key to the index entry. Should the illustrative material be *unrelated* to the accompanying text (as would be true of maps in a travel guide), the key term for the entry head is supplied from the legend (caption or table head, as the case may be). (For different ways to designate page keys to illustrative material, see chapter 5, ''Style.'')

Text supplement entry copy. Whether and how extensively supplements to the text—such as appendices, notes, and glossary—should be indexed is a decision to be made early; this is clearly impossible if the proof is delivered in batches. The index may only suggest the scope of appendices, or it may cover them in detail. Certain texts, by reason of conciseness or uninterrupted continuity (for example, one based on documents), may relegate all supporting data to the appendices. Such appendices must be indexed thoroughly. Extensive notes containing significant detail at the end of the text rather than footnoted (a design choice supported by economy) also require indexing. Whereas a footnote of special importance (that is, containing information *not* simply supporting what is in the text) may be identified by the page number and *n* (15n), notes at the end of the text must be indexed in the same way as the text. (See chapter 5, ''Style,'' for specific detail.)

Names entry copy. Indexing names of persons satisfies several needs: (1) specific identification (for example, by showing relationships within families) along with alternate spellings, pseudonyms, and so on; and (2) text reference–source correlation. Whether names should be included in the subject index or constitute a separate index depends, first of all, on the publisher's policy. A publisher with a list limited to reports of scientific research may find a single index preferable to multiple indexes. Indexing names to be part of a single index is integrated with indexing concepts. However, to make sure that spelling error does not creep in, a complete entry should be worked up *every time* a name appears and the spelling (including accents) rechecked on the spot; when the entries are alphabetized, the correlation invariably turns up typographical error.

A separate names index (which may be an author index combined with a title index) is desirable when (1) the number of indexable names in the text exceeds an arbitrary number (say, over 300), or (2) the names index is really a key to text and note references to sources. In the first instance—in, for example, a work on history, biography, or literature—the researcher is aided by having the names (and, when applicable, titles of works) separate from the index to concepts. In the second instance, the researcher's main concern is to find citations to the work of specific colleagues on specific research investigations. The technique for preparing a names (author) index serving as a *key to sources*—whether the names are included in the subject index or are in a separate names index—is one of the most important for any indexer working in science.

The point of departure for a names index is *not* the citation on the text page but the reference source in the list of references or bibliographic notes. The technique is *not* to correlate the reference with the text but to correlate the text citation with the reference.

The first step is to index the names in the list of references, preferably chapter by chapter. These names (including initials) with page numbers are typed up on strips (sheets). Using the list of references (bibliographic notes) for correlation, the text pages are scanned for source reference data (superscript number, author name, etc.), and the appropriate page number key is added to the typed-up list of names. In this process, discrepancies between the spelling of names in the text and in the list of references become obtrusive. Other discrepancies will become apparent when the typed-up list of names is alphabetized in the final preparation of a names index. For references with multiple authors, not all the names need be indexed. A reference with two authors should carry both names in the names index. A reference with more than two authors should carry only the name of the principal (first) author in the names index.

Title entry copy. Title entries may be (1) included in a subject index, (2) combined with a names (author) index, or (3) presented as a separate title index. In the first instance, the titles are few or only of supplementary interest. In the second instance, the work is often a critique, as in comparative literature. In the third instance, the work is usually a collection, as of verse or songs, in which case there may be an overlap with an index of first lines. (See following section.) The publisher may choose to substitute a detailed table of contents for an index when the collection is by a single author. For either of the separate indexes as described in (2) and (3), the *title* and *author* entries are best prepared as a separate operation. In this technique, material for the subject index is *ignored* as the pages are scanned and titles prepared as entries (along with names or first lines for a combined index).

Copy is also worked up for cross-references to alternative titles, including original titles in foreign languages or the translation of foreign-language titles. A title index for the works of one person (the subject of a critique or a biography, for example) should not include titles (and authors) other than for the subject of the work. In this case, the title index for the subject of the work must be prepared with special care: the titles for the separate index must be plainly distinguished from the titles (and authors) incidental to the main subject. Such incidental titles (and authors) should be incorporated in the subject index and hence prepared with it. Once the title entry copy for a separate index is completed, it should be put aside for alphabetizing and editing when the subject index (including the incidental title and author entries just described) is finished. Invariably, in the preparation of the subject index entries, the indexer will find titles that have been overlooked. Inconsistency in spelling and the use of particles or accents in titles will turn up as the entries are alphabetized, a matter that should be called to the publisher's immediate attention. It should be noted that for any work other than a collection by, or critique of, a single author, a title entry must appear in two places in an index: under the author's name and as a separate entry.

First lines entry. For a collection of verse or songs, titles are often in the form of first lines. First line titles may also be incidental entries in a subject index. Two important concerns in preparing such index entries are working up copy to conform with the publisher's policy on (1) alphabetization (whether introductory articles are heeded, ignored, or inverted); and (2) style (whether to follow the original precisely with respect to capitalization and so on, or to restyle the original). (See chapters 4 and 5 for recommendations.)

Legal cases entry copy. References to legal sources are often in notes, which may amplify a legal reference in the text or introduce the citation for the first time. These legal references may be incorporated in a subject index or set up as a table of cases. In either instance the entries should be worked up as a separate procedure.

The first step is to type up copy for the cases referred to in the text and those in the notes (footnotes) chapter by chapter. This copy should be rechecked to ensure that a citation in a footnote but *not* also in the text is coded as a footnote (*n*). Once completed, the list of entries should be reviewed and supplemented with alternative forms generated from the original citation, that is, the case should be indexed under both the plaintiff and the defendant:

Smith v. Jones
Jones, Smith v.

(See also chapter 4, ''Alphabetization and Order''; chapter 5, ''Style.'')

Cross-reference entry copy. Two preparations to be made *early* in indexing are critical to accurate and informative cross-references: (1) establishing preferred terminology for equivalent terms (that is, synonyms, acronyms, abbreviations, and alternative spellings), the basis for external cross-references; and (2) projecting a pattern for entry heads in terms of both general and specific aspects of concepts, the basis for internal cross-references.

In anticipating external cross-references, familiarity with the subject matter of the text will alert the indexer to possible alternative usages and the one(s) to be preferred. With this stimulus in mind, the indexer should write up cross-references whenever alternative usages occur. In a text with different *spellings* for alternative usages—and it does happen—the cross-reference(s) may be ''duplicated'' a number of times. Alphabetization will reveal these alternative spellings and other discrepancies that must be cleaned up in index editing and styling.

Clues to needed internal cross-references surface when the index pattern is being formulated as a methodology is projected. An internal cross-reference is *always* from a general to a specific aspect of a concept: Bird. *See also* Robin. *Not*: Robin. *See also* Bird.

As material for entries on *general* aspects of a concept are being gleaned from the text, amplifications and details (specifics) that need to be indexed become *modifications* or *separate entries*. It such specific aspects of a concept are inappropriate as modifications, a cross-reference from the general to the specific is written up. At the same time, the specific aspect of the concept is treated in a separate entry. Thus text material on *bird* and the species *robin* is indexed as: Bird, Robin; and Bird. *See also* Robin.

ENTRY CHECKING

Entry checking—comparing the accumulated entries against the marked text—is a simple task, particularly if continuous strips or sheets (instead of cards) are used for the original copy. Error found during entry checking is not the sort to be found during index editing after entries are alphabetized. Entry checking turns up wrong or missing page numbers, wrong inclusive page numbers, misspellings, duplicate entries under different key words—a multitude of little errors that, if not found now, will cause irritation and frustration later when suspicion of error leads to a frantic attempt to find out why and where it happened.

The benefit of checking index entries on continuous strips (rather than separate cards) is obvious. In checking the copy prepared on the strips against the text, needed alterations over a succession of pages may be quickly seen. Although cards may be laid out in a column for similar checking, the range of visibility is limited. When the index has been prepared from galleys—the galleys being "paged" when page proof is available—the checking operation may be combined with the addition of the page numbers to the already prepared copy.

For an index prepared on cards, a supplementary technique for spot checking is to slowly ruffle the cards to expose the page numbers, which should be consecutive. Typographical error will also be revealed.

During the checking procedure, *text error*—found during entry preparation or turned up now—is gleaned: typographical error, inconsistency in the spelling of names and in dates and other numerical data, wrongly identified figures or tables, factual blunders, and grammatical and stylistic faults. A list of these errors may be sent to the publisher as soon as the checking is finished or—since other error may be discovered during alphabetization and editing—submitted along with the index manuscript. (A publisher may want to process the index manuscript and corrections at the same time.) This procedure of text error discovery and submission to the publisher used to be just another routine in index preparation. However, current composition technology that features photocopies of page layouts for index preparation seriously hinders this task: the material for indexing is often far from being final and may go through a number of additional proofings, error corrections, and layout changes before being ready for press. Hence, the indexer's list of text errors may not only be excessive but may also duplicate errors being taken care of at the publishing house. Also, if the indexer is fighting a deadline, screening proof for error may have to be bypassed. As a substitute, inconsistencies in names, numerical data, and styling may be indicated on the index manuscript. (See subsequent section on manuscript checking.)

ALPHABETIZATION

Writers on indexing and publisher's guides for indexers differ about a methodology for alphabetization, mainly about when it should be done. One "school" of indexers attempts to soften the rigors of indexing detail by proposing that alphabetization (particularly when indexing with cards) should be interspersed with entry copy preparation. This methodology makes *impossible* the kind of control that the indexer needs over all aspects of the job, such as the checking for error just described. Whenever a question of error or inconsistency arises, index entry copy has to be in consecutive order for efficient comparison with text proof; this is possible only when the continuity of prepared copy is maintained until the last minute. Alphabetization should not be undertaken until copy preparation is complete and entries are checked.

From the beginning the indexer should have firmly in mind whether the indexing is to be word by word or letter by letter, as well as other principles of order that need to be incorporated in the alphabetizing procedure. The refining of alphabetization and order occurs with index editing and styling.

EDITING AND STYLING

Up to this point the indexer has worked to get the index copy to reflect the concepts extracted from the text (See chapter 1, "Methodology"). The prepared index entries should (1) be in conformity with the index pattern selected after analysis of the text and (2) be arranged (alphabetized and otherwise ordered) according to the rules for indexes for this particular subject and format. The index is now ready to be edited and styled.

In general, the aims of editing are (1) substantive, having to do with entry content as related to index format, and (2) mechanical, having to do with spelling, typography, and punctuation (one aspect of styling). Styling for production (marking up the index for the compositor) is concerned with the structuring of the index to show the proper relationships between entries and between entries and modifications and cross-references. (See Figure 2.)

Technique. As is true of all steps in index preparation, the more the indexer can *see* of the materials being handled (whether proof or index copy), the more likely is the index to be accurate and well structured. To prepare for this phase of the work, *groups* of alphabetized entries should be placed in vertical rows. The extent of the display should be as large as possible in terms of related entries. For example, a major heading of *Chicken* in a cookbook should have spread out below it all the modifications and cross-references for that head. By this means the indexer can readily see what needs

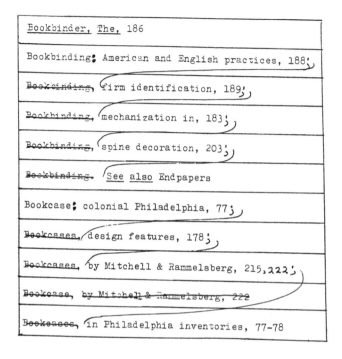

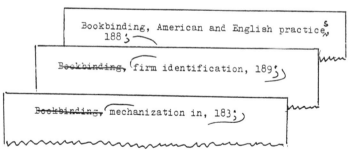

Figure 2. Index editing: a comparison of copy on gummed strips and on cards.

to be done to the whole entry in terms of format, the details of modifications, and the validity of cross-references.

Entry content and organization. In editing index entries for content in relation to the predetermined index pattern, two matters need to be considered: (1) What is there and how is it organized? and (2) what may be elsewhere that (a) duplicates or (b) is an alternative approach to the concept(s) covered in the entry at hand? Has what should have been left out been left out, and has what should have been included been included?

The discovery of a deviation from the predetermined pattern may require restructuring the entry at hand and, often, related entries. For example, in a cookbook index the entry *Custard* may have modifications of *baked, boiled, caramel,* and *pie.* There is an obvious omission of *chocolate.* This discovery leads to a search for implicated entries: not only *chocolate* but *egg,* and so on. And under these heads the indexer should find (under both *Chocolate* and *Egg*) the modification *custard.* In sum, editing does not involve just the prepared entries displayed; it may require referring to and altering entries alphabetically ordered elsewhere. Terminology and page numbers must also be consistent. Passages *remote* from each other in the text will only come together when the index is alphabetized and ordered; here terminology may be inconsistent and will need to be altered. For example, again in a cookbook under *Chocolate* the entry may show both *beverages* and *drinks;* these modifications need to be combined.

There is a difference between a alternative approach to a concept and *entry redundancy.* A redundant entry duplicates all or part of the concepts indexed under a preferred term elsewhere in the index. For example, part of the concepts relating to *Poultry* might be under that entry head and others under *Fowl.* The copy under *Fowl* should be combined with that under *Poultry,* and perhaps a cross-reference set up: Fowl. *See* Poultry.

Modifications. Editing and styling an index entry are mainly concerned with modifications; it is impossible to project the final form of modifications as index copy is being prepared, since decisions made when indexing one part of the text may differ from those made for another. The aims of modification editing are: (1) achieving internal pattern consistency in keeping with the predetermined pattern for the index; (2) eliminating unnecessary modifications by combining page numbers for synonymous terms under the term preferred (for example, *Soviet* rather than *Russian*); (3) eliminating the modification altogether if the information in the modification is not significant and the page references for the entry head are few (less than six or seven); (4) eliminating modifications that are legitimate entry heads, with the provision of cross-references; (5) eliminating all but the absolutely essential sub-modifications and sub-sub-modifications.

While uniformity in modification structure is not mandatory (for example, the rigid inclusion of prepositions for all modifications when such inclusion is needed for only a few), consistency in the grammatical *form* of the modification is desirable. An entry on *Cooking methods* should be edited to get conformity among modifications prepared as: *to simmer, broiling, stews,* etc.

The key word in a modification should be brought forward, so that the researcher moves with ease from the key word in the entry head to the key word in the modification. However, inversions in modifications are *not* necessary and only irritate the researcher in trying to get a quick fix on a key to information in the text. Also contributing to this end is the elimination of all superfluous words.

Cross-references. Both kinds of cross-references—external and internal—have specific requirements. (Recall an external cross-reference is from one *equivalent* head to another—the head, or term, that is most likely to be looked up. An internal cross-reference is from an entry dealing with a general—as distinct from a specific—aspect of a concept to those specific aspects.)

An important task in entry checking, entry editing and styling, and manuscript proofing is the validation of cross-references: discovering and eliminating *blind* cross-references and reviewing all cross-references as properly external or internal and styling accordingly. There is always the possibility that additional cross-references will be needed from alternative spellings and synonyms that were not provided when the entry copy was prepared. Also, rearrangements to satisfy the index pattern requirements may alter the original decisions about cross-references.

The indexer cannot be sure that all blind cross-references (for example, from a singular construction to a plural, or vice versa) will be discovered until the final proofing of copy. When an index is prepared on cards that are to go into composition, cross-references should be *rechecked* after alphabetizing and editing and styling are finished. Even then a further check of index proof for error in cross-references will often prove to be productive.

Since multiple indexes (for example, for subject, titles, authors, and first lines) are prepared separately, editing cross-references should include a cross check among the different indexes.

MANUSCRIPT PREPARATION

When the publisher wants the index to be submitted as manuscript on 8 1/2″ by 11″ sheets, the manuscript should be double-spaced, with one column to a sheet. Space should be left between the letters of the alphabet. The continuity of the developing index should be rechecked as it is typed up. Innumerable minor errors, and some major ones, are caught in this way: errors in spelling, preferred terminology, alphabetization, and page numbers.

A publisher may require electronic index manuscript, consisting of a disk compatible with the firm's system and one or more printouts. If the indexer is not equipped for turning out such manuscript, yet wishes to retain the client's business, manuscript preparation may be subcontracted to a word-processor operator.

Indexing to space. When a publisher wants an index written to space, that is, to fill a specified number of book pages, he must supply the indexer with the number of characters per index line and the number of index lines per column (and page).

A guide for comparing manuscript lines against the space allocated to the printed index is provided by the distribution of letters in alphabetized works (for example, encyclopedias): one fourth for A through C, one fourth for D through M, one fourth for N through P, and one fourth for Q through Z. If the line count is over in any one of these divisions, adjustments may be made in succeeding divisions by tightening copy. If the line count is consistently *under* that projected for the index manuscript and the indexing has been adequate, the publisher should be notified before the index is padded out just to fill space. Often adjustments can be made in composition and production: a larger type face, fewer lines per column, and space added between letter breaks (See chapter 6, "Production.")

MANUSCRIPT CHECKING

One might thank that, with all the attention to detail required up to and through manuscript preparation, the end product could be shipped off without delay. Such is not the case. No index manuscript is without error, often discovered just before it is wrapped up for delivery. The aim of checking at this stage is to make a final effort to ensure accuracy—not to make up for conceptual failings.

Four features should be checked methodically: cross-references, page numbers, alphabetization (or other order), and spelling of proper names and unusual terms. Several of these operations go hand in hand. Although styling inconsistency is also noted, styling is not the primary concern: styling error can be picked up as each copy sheet is scanned in a final salute to the finished index.

In a cross-reference check, each standing internal and external cross-reference is actually verified. If this checking procedure is done first, the eye will pick up incidental error in page numbers. (If the comparison between entry copy and text has been conscientious, page number errors at this stage should be mainly those introduced in typing: transpositions, omissions, improper form for inclusive numbers, and styling defects for tables and illustrations.) Alphabetization check should be a separate operation; incidental spelling error will be picked up at the same time. A final verification of proper names and unusual terms unfortunately often reveals error, especially in foreign language and scientific texts.

IN-HOUSE PROCEDURE

Any index *not* written in-house but by an author or freelancer is unpredictable, the exception being when the in-house editor and freelancer have had a long-term satisfactory relationship. The quality of the index determines what has to be done in-house. An unsatisfactory index by an author presents unattractive alternatives: (1) take a chance and try to salvage a bad job; (2) get a professional indexer to write a new index if there is time.

An index that is to be salvaged should be given first aid, not subjected to major surgery. Significant defects may be eliminated by the following procedure:

To test for accuracy, every tenth to fifteenth index entry should be checked against the text for (1) content, (2) spelling, and (3) page numbers. If the errors are few and minor, they should be corrected. If the faults are major, the index may have to be discarded.

The next step is to check usage, index arrangement, and index styling. An index written by a professional who knows the publisher's style preferences should present few problems of arrangement and style. However, if the index copy is sent to the author for approval and revision, the author's changes may introduce serious defects in the index pattern: blind cross-references, inconsistent terminology changes, and pattern alterations that throw the index out of balance. *Every change made by an author should be verified by comparing it with the text.*

Index terminology should reflect the text; if the manuscript has been edited for accuracy and consistency in usage, problems of terminology should not arise during index editing. Such is not always the case. The best approach to eliminating terminology defects is to spot check proper names, scientific terms, and nondictionary terms (neologisms). This task should not be put off, since error and inconsistency may have to be corrected in the printed text as well as in the index. Names selected for checking should be those with multiple page numbers; by this means the most noticeable errors are likely to be discovered. At the same time given (Christian) names may be added when missing. Inversions that do not reflect the text or standard usage should also be corrected.

A *separate* operation in index editing is the cross-reference check. The blind cross-reference leads the searcher nowhere; what he or she is supposed to *see* simply does not exist. A cross-reference may also be circuitous, leading the searcher from one unrewarding stop to another. Also, the form of the cross-reference may not agree with the term referred to. Accordingly, *every* cross-reference should be checked against the index entry it refers to. Also a cross-reference to a single heading—that is, a single term with page number(s)—squanders that user's time. The cross-reference should be eliminated and the page numbers keyed to both entries.

An alphabetization check is another separate operation. Since there are alternative methods—letter by letter and word by word—and different policies about handling particles, the system used for each index should be known and followed.

How many page numbers may be keyed to any one index entry? One standard is that any term in an index followed by more than seven page numbers should be modified. The nature of the subject matter may liberalize this figure, since nothing is gained by supplying modifications simply to meet an arbitrary standard.

When there is no justification for more than the standard for page numbers following any one entry, the author may be given a choice of eliminating page numbers or providing modifications.

Checking index style is the last operation in index editing; setting a pattern on a style sheet for each index is useful to eliminate inconsistency, since styles differ for indexes as well as among indexers. The style sheet should include style for punctuation and cross-references as a minimum.

EQUIVALENCE TECHNIQUES

In indexing, as in any job where workers, materials, and time must be synchronized, one factor out of "time" can bring the whole process to an abrupt halt. It is usually the materials factor—unavailability of page proof because of disruptions in the movement of text copy to and through composition, with consequent delay in the delivery of page proof to the indexer.

The solution to the problem is to write the index from galley, and then translate the galley proof into "page" proof by an equivalence technique, that is, the translation of one type format for a bounded passage into another type format: to turn what you have to work with into what is needed for composition. The *physical* equivalence between type on the galley proof and the same text on the to-be-delivered page proof make it possible to "page" the galleys. Until pages are ready, index entries are prepared from galley. Then when page proof is delivered, the equivalent page-type area is marked on the galleys and numbered. The page numbers for the entries falling within that area are then added to the already prepared copy. (Index entries for illustrations and tables must be worked up separately after page proof is delivered.)

Another problem with indexing materials occurs with a major blunder in page makeup—passages or pages left out or in the wrong sequence, changes in page design, or changes in the location of illustrations and tables. Obviously, this blunder means changes in the index, about which the indexer must be informed. The publisher may try to do so by phone or letter. If the changes are minor, the indexer may have enough information to make corrections. The only safe guide, however, is revised page proof, either marked for remake or remade. With these proofs in hand, the indexer *repages* (*refolios*) the *previous* proof and changes the pages numbers on the index entry copy.

For a work to be published both in English and as a *translation,* two indexes are needed. Except in the unusual circumstances when the indexer is also a linguist, the translator must be given material for adapting the English index to an index for translation. Two differences are important: (1) the type area for the same text passage will (in most instances) be *larger* in the translation than in the English version; (2) the alphabetization will have no equivalence. For the translator to adapt the English index, he or she needs the equivalent page numbers for the translation. Index entries for the English version are prepared and checked but *not* alphabetized. The English text page proof is then *repaged* (*refolioed*) to match the page proof of the translation; these page numbers are then added to a *copyprint* of the sheets of the English index entries. (Indexing on sheets, not cards, is the preferred method for dual-language indexes.) Heads and subheads and paragraphing in the translation give the indexer almost all the guidance needed for repaging the index entries (adding page numbers from the translation) on the copyprint. With the copyprint of the index entries on sheets to work with, the translator turns the English version into its foreign-language equivalent. This done, the translator (or indexer) prepares (alphabetizes, etc.) the translated version for composition. The indexer also completes the English version of the index.

Index *manuscript* preparation from *galley proof* is seldom needed. However, the indexer (who may be the author) may be unavailable for completing an index if there is an inordinate delay in providing page proof for an index started on galley. (This dilemma is hard to justify, but it does occur.) The technique is to turn the galleys into theoretically equivalent pages. Using the book design for type lines to a page as a base, the galleys are divided into approximate equivalents, as "page" 1-a, 1-b, 1-c for a book with approximately three pages to the galley. This equivalence is not precise; although accurate boundaries will be found for chapters, the design requirements for spacing for heads and subheads within chapters make galley-page equivalence only approximate. Manuscript is prepared with the galley keys (1-a, 1-b, and 1-c) to represent the page numbers. When page proof is available, the galleys are *repaged* (*refolioed*) to establish the equivalence. Then with the completed index manuscript at hand, the ''page'' numbers from the galleys are converted into the equivalent page proof numbers, entry by entry. This is an arduous job; a preferable alternative is for the publisher to use the editorial staff to complete the index from galleys.

MULTIVOLUME INDEXES

An index for a multivolume work (an encyclopedia or other work published as a set) has requirements beyond those for an index for a one-volume work. The very bulk of the matter to be handled (in terms of both text proof and indexing materials) and the time factor (months may be needed to prepare such an index, with intense pressure for delivery as the deadline approaches) make any multivolume index a major undertaking. To control indexing materials and meet production goals, indexing a multivolume work is in most instances feasible only as a team operation, either in-house or at an indexing service.

Such an index may be handled in a number of ways. The critical factor is planning. When such planning is bypassed on a crash publishing project, the result can be most unwelcome reviews. Planning for a multivolume index involves: (1) materials handling, (2) selecting and training personnel, (3) establishing a methodology and technique, and (4) projecting production deadlines. For cumulative indexes and similar publications (such as an index for a major newspaper) these prerequisites are in place. For a *new* multivolume publication each of these factors needs to be integrated into a total work plan. (Some differences in the details of work organization and storage of files for revision apply in computer-assisted indexing, but the basics of methodology and technique are the same for all multivolume indexes.)

Materials handling. For a multivolume index, setting up a permanent card file that can be revised is the only sensible approach. The cards should be of good quality, such as will withstand handling for a number of revisions. They should be housed in metal boxes with sturdy alphabetical dividers. One person should be responsible for the physical maintenance of the file and for alphabetization and other ordering (such as that preliminary to a revision). Spot revisions, such as a text correction for the next printing, not the next revision, should also be made by the person in charge of the file. The reason for this strict delegation of responsibility is that any permanent index file open to a number of hands is going to become disordered, then considered useless, and then abandoned. (It is not the nature of a publishing house to preserve the old—whether manuscript, proof, or books; rather, on with the new!). Accordingly, special effort must be made to maintain any permanent file.

As is true for any index prepared on cards *for composition,* the cards are numbered on the face (preferably with a numbering machine) *after* alphabetization. When the cards are to be used for a revision they are *resorted by page number;* another set of consecutive numbers is stamped on the *back* of the cards *before alphabetization* but after checking and editing. By this means the file may also be maintained by order of page numbers.

The same basic principles apply to handling proof for a multi-volume index as for a single-volume index. Such proof comes in batches from production. Control procedures are receiving, checking, logging in, and distributing to the indexers. One person should be responsible. The most likely candidate is a clerk typist, particularly if a typist is part of the team for entry preparation.

Personnel. As noted before, a multivolume index is feasible only as a team operation, in the house or at an indexing service. An indexing service is usually experienced in such indexing and large enough to assign personnel full-time to the project. The in-house staff should expect to be called on for consultation and to edit the finished work.

An in-house multivolume indexing project is less of a strain if the publication is major (an encyclopedia) or is one of a number of on-going multivolume publications undergoing continuous revision, and *if* there is a central indexing staff responsible for all indexing. Such a firm is able to recruit and train a permanent staff. If the multivolume work is new and has an uncertain future with respect to the need for, and time of, revisions, the indexing staff must be acknowledged to be temporary; recruitment and training are consequently difficult.

The following discussion details an approach to a new multivolume index; however, the principles are valid for any multivolume project.

The keys to a successful multivolume index project are standardization and simplification. Before any work is undertaken, a guide should be prepared specifying standards for index format, style, alphabetization and order, and terminology.

The size of the multivolume work and the schedule for text proof delivery determine the number of indexers and ancillary personnel needed and when they should be employed. A steady and significant flow of pages for indexing (proof or copyprints of made-up pages) should be assured before indexers report for work.

METHODOLOGY AND TECHNIQUE

Since an index to a multivolume work is usually published in a separate volume, index length is not so critical as it is when an index must be fitted into the format of a single volume. However, the number of index *items* per page (*not* index *entries*) should be determined so that the output of different indexers can be balanced. Over-indexing by one indexer and under-indexing by another will distort both concept coverage and the index pattern when the output of different workers is assembled. Interim deadlines for index copy preparation should be set up in relation to the projected schedule for text proof delivery and the deadline for delivery of the completed index to production. By leapfrog assignments, a check is possible of worker production. For example, distributing proof in batches of 50 pages to each indexer and keeping track of when the work is completed will indicate what is a reasonable work load. If three indexers are employed, position A indexer would be assigned pages 1 through 50, 151 through 200, and so on. Indexer B would be assigned pages 51 through 100, 201 through 250, and so on. And indexer C would pick up with pages 101 through 150.

Since no two indexers approach an indexing task in exactly the same way, there is always the risk that index items won't mix when entries are finally assembled. As a safeguard, specific clues to key terms should be included in the indexers' guidance, depending on the nature of the multivolume work: heads, subheads, tables, illustrations, proper terms, introductions to chapters and sections, summaries, and references.

If the work is to have a separate names index, it may be

expedient to assign that task to one person, working with a duplicate set of text proof.

With a team operation, there are two approaches to copy preparation: the indexers may type up the index items on cards, or they may mark the proof for a typist. In the latter instance, the same communication signals must be used by all indexers. Typed-up cards should be checked both for typographical error and for conformity to the standards set for the particular index. An in-house editor is the only choice for the task if egos are not to be bruised.

Alphabetization of a multivolume index may be safely assigned to the in-house clerical staff, some members always seeming to have down time. To save time, the editor checking the prepared index items should follow on the heels of the typist, and the alphabetizing clerks should follow on the heels of the editor.

For finally styling and editing, each editor should be given leapfrog assignments of letters to even out the work load, since some letters will have more entries than others. A final review of the prepared index should be done by the in-house editor. A most important feature of this review is verification of cross-references.

When it comes to meeting production deadlines on a multivolume index, prayer and pressure are just not enough. In the first place, the deadlines must be realistic and consistent with the preparation of an acceptable index. Second, the air in the production schedule must be fairly distributed between editorial and production if each is to stay alive when the going gets rough. Moreover, the panic potential can be minimized by establishing and *checking up on* interim production commitments, for page proof delivery to the indexers as well as each indexer's output.

SUMMARY

Chapter 1 covered the methodology of indexing: planning and strategy and tactics for index entry construction. The succession of maneuvers needed to effect the methodology plan comprises indexing technique. Except for computer-assisted indexing, indexing materials are few and inexpensive: a receptacle for page proof, cards or gummed sheets, a typewriter, boxes for filing cards or strips, and the furnishings of an ordinary desk (paper clips, pens, scissors, etc.) However, the organization and control of materials affect job efficiency: hundreds of small pieces (single entries) accumulate during the indexing process; misplacing or losing parts weakens the very foundation on which the index is built.

From time to time an indexing technique is proposed that makes indexing "easy," all aimed at bypassing the constraints of "piece-work." Suffice it to say, none of these slick methods ever works. Although differences exist among indexers in the choice of materials and equipment and in minor details of the indexing procedure, a standard technique for entry construction is generally accepted.

Following a preliminary survey of the text and formulation of a methodology, work on an index is entirely a matter of making individual entries, styled according to a standard, and fashioned so that each "brick" fits into the projected index design (format). Along the way decisions are made about preferred terminology and needed cross-references.

With entry construction completed, the actual work on building the index begins. Entries are alphabetized and otherwise ordered. Entries on individual concepts (terms) thus brought together are blended and refined. Terminology is finalized and additional cross-references are provided as needed. This work of combination, elimination, and integration completed, the index is ready to be turned into manuscript copy (or a computer printout) for composition.

Changing indexing routines may be needed when (1) the compositor is unable to deliver page proof on schedule, (2) when a major blunder is found in page makeup *after* the index copy is finished, and (3) when two versions of an index are required, one in English and the other in translation. In each instance an *equivalence* technique may be used to resolve the difficulty. A most arduous indexing assignment, and one calling for major innovations in technique, is that requiring an index when *no* proof is available. This means the index must be written from manuscript.

Preparing an index for a multivolume work—an encyclopedia, for example—differs little in technique from that for single-volume indexing. The difference is in planning and control of materials. Since a number of workers are usually involved, the work must be carefully organized to ensure equality in work assignments and conformity to a single standard for entry construction, terminology, format, and style.

CHAPTER 3

FORMAT

Index format is the media of the message. It is hard to think of anything quite as useless as the words of an index without the format. Its purpose is to organize and display the results of the processes described in chapter 1 ("Methodology") and chapter 2 ("Technique").

Although certain features of the format favor different disciplines (e.g., science or humanities), *how the index looks* should depend almost entirely upon the author's presentation of the subject matter and only secondarily upon penchants of the indexer.

Details of index design (head, inversions, modifications, sub-modifications, cross-references, and page numbers) unfold as concepts are gleaned from the text and manipulated to expose relationships between elements of the author's thesis. Variations in format schemes are few: line-by-line or paragraphed (run-in) organization, word-by-word or letter-by-letter alphabetization, inclusive or noninclusive page numbers. Such adjustments as are needed occur when complex terms in combination call for innovations and are more often a matter of style then of format.

As has been suggested, certain subjects and disciplines are better suited to certain formats than to others. The humanities seem to fit well into the paragraphed patterns, while the sciences do well with the line-by-line pattern. A social science text with a mathematical or research bent adapts to the line-by-line format, while such works of a theoretical nature fit the paragraphed form.

The best value for the available space is obtained with the paragraphed pattern. On the other hand, when the text is slight and bulk is needed for a book, the line-by-line format offers an advantage.

Consistency in an index pattern for all the basic structural elements is not only desirable but also critical in attaining index integrity for the benefit of the index user. On the other hand, *forced* consistency in the use of such minor elements as particles and grammatical forms is more a hindrance than a help. As has been already noted, an index is *not* to be read and, not being textural matter, is not subject to grammatical and syntactical rules.

DISTINCTIVE FEATURES

In this section the distinctive features of index format will be defined (with synonyms) and alternative treatment given with examples.

An index has structure. The basic elements of that structure are: (1) an alphabetical arrangement of (2) entries (3) keyed by page numbers (or another system) and (4) supplemented with cross-references. These elements may be placed in the format (design) in different ways.

Entry: The total element in an index design that satisfies the searcher, that is, points to the idea (concept) he or she is looking for and where to find it in the text. An entry consists of a head alone or supplemented with modifications and perhaps sub-modifications and cross-references.

Modification: As the term implies, a qualification of the concept covered by the entry head. A qualification of a modification is a sub-modification. Synonyms are *subentry* (*subhead*) and *subsubentry* (*subsubhead*); these terms indicate position, not function.

Head (heading): A keyword or phrase introducing the entry and determining the alphabetical order. The format for a head varies not only according to the pattern (line by line or paragraphed) but also according to (1) index conventions for alphabetization and order (e.g., inversion) and the need for (2) modifications, (3) submodifications, and (4) cross-references.

1. Conventional constructs for a head are: (a) noun, (b) adjective plus noun or noun modifier plus noun, but (c) *never adjective alone.*

a. Bomb, 00
b. Atomic (or atom) bomb, 00
c. *Never* Atomic (as head)
    bomb, 00 (modification)
    energy, 00 (modification)
        or
    Atomic: bomb, 00; energy, 00

Inversion. An alteration in a heading phrase of adjective plus noun or noun modifier plus noun to place the key word first. A pure inversion (see below) is never needed in a modification or submodification. The principle of an inversion is best shown by the line-by-line pattern:

Andrew Jackson inverted becomes: *Jackson, Andrew*
Battle of Waterloo inverted becomes: *Waterloo, Battle of*
    Such concepts should *never* be set up as:

Jackson   or   Waterloo
    Andrew   Battle of

This raises the question of the difference between an inversion and a modification. As just shown, a pure inversion is limited to *one line*. A modification may be on the same line as the head when it is the *only* modification or on a separate line with multiple modifications:

Energy, atomic (one modification)
Energy
    atomic
    mechanical

(See also chapter 4, "Alphabetization and Order.")
    Conventions of *order* affect the head format when the index covers homographs; the format depends on the alphabetical (sometimes chronological) order of the term that differentiates the head:

Organ (anatomy)
Organ (instrument)
    or

Smith, John (1801–1879)
Smith, John (1820–1890)
Smith, John (1840–1900)

The same devices is useful when concepts have definite subclasses that are given extensive treatment in the text. In the example, the subject *leukemia* is discussed extensively by itself and in both the *acute* and *chronic* forms:

Leukemia,
   modification,
Leukemia (acute)
   modification,
Leukemia (chronic)
   modification,

Cross-reference. A pointer from a synonym (or another alternative term) to guide the searcher to the heading where the concept sought is indexed. An external cross-reference directs the searcher from the entry at hand to an exact equivalent. The directive is given in the form of *See* . . . . An internal cross-reference directs the searcher from the entry at hand to some subdivision of the entry concept. The directive is given in the form of *See also* . . . .
For both the line-by-line and the paragraphed pattern, an external cross-reference follows the head:

Head. *See* . . . .

Internal cross-references serve two distinct purposes: to direct the searcher (1) from the entry head to a subdivision of the entry concept, or (2) from a modification or sub-modification to such a subdivision. For the line-by-line pattern, the possible forms are:

Head. *See also* . . . .
Head, 00. *See also* . . . .
      or
Head, 00
  modification, 00
  modification, 00
  See also . . . .

Head, 00
    modification, 00. *See also* . . . .
      sub-modification, 00. *See also* . . . .

The paragraphed pattern for indexes is less adaptable to the use of cross-references than the line-by-line pattern. External cross-references follow the head, but internal cross-references have no convenient place to go but the end of the entry:

Head. *See* . . . .
Head, 00; modification, 000; modification, 000
    See also . . . .

If absolutely necessary, an internal cross-reference may be enclosed in parentheses after the head or a modification, but the practice is clumsy with respect to styling:

Head, 00 (*see also*. . . .); modification, 00
Head, 00; modification, 0000; modification, 000
    (*see also*. . . .); modification, 0000

(See also chapter 5, "Style.")

The main format patterns for an index entry are: (1) line by line (entry a line or indented), (2) paragraphed (run-in or run-on), and (3) mixed.

(1) The line-by-line pattern requires that each head and modification begin on a separate line, the exception being an entry head with a single modification. (Some firms also permit the format in the third example.) A cross-reference may follow the head, a modification, or the end of the entry (see section on cross-references).

Head, 00
  modification, 00
    sub-modification,00
Head, modification, 00
Head, modification, 00
  modification, 00

(2) The paragraphed pattern requires that the modifications follow the head, the type being run on line by line. A cross-

reference comes at the end of the entry, or it may be placed in parentheses within the entry (see section on cross-references).

> Head, 00; modification, 00; modification, 00;
>   modification, 00
> Head: modification, 00

Note: For sub-modifications within the paragraphed pattern see subsequent discussion on modifications.

(3) A mixed (modified) line-by-line pattern permits major modification categories to be paragraphed for the more efficient handling of submodifications.

> Head, 00
>   modification, 00
>   modification, 00; sub-modification, 00; sub-modification, 00

A similar device is available for the paragraphed pattern: Instead of a *continuous* run-in style, modifications begin on separate lines preceded by an em dash, sub-modifications being run in.

> Head, 00
> —modification; sub-modifications, 00; sub-modification,
>   00; sub-modification, 00
> —modification, 00; sub-modification, 00; sub-modification, 00
> —modification, 00

In the line-by-line pattern the principal decisions with respect to modifications and sub-modifications have to do with spacing. The following examples show the different design possibilities. Those preceded by an asterisk are not recommended.

> *Single modification*

> Head, modification, 000

> *Multiple modifications*

> Head, 000 *or* Head *or* Head:
>   modification, 000

```
        modification, 000
        (Indentation—1 em)
   * Head, modification, 000 or Head: modification, 000
        modification, 000
        modification, 000
        (Indentation—1 em)


            or


   Head, 000
        modification, 000
        modification, 000
        (Indentation—2 em)
```

Runovers are spaced as follows:

```
   Head, 000
        modification
          runover, 000
        modification, 000
          sub-modification
             runover, 000
   (Indention—2 em)
```

Sub-modifications
```
   Head, 000
        modification, 000
          sub-modification, 000
   * Head, modification, 000
        modification, 000
             sub-modification, 000
        (Indentation of submodification—1 em)
```

A mixed pattern for the paragraphed format has been described. The problem of miscellaneous sub-modifications in a pure paragraphed format is not easily solved. A useful device is to repeat the modifying term to differentiate sub-modifications:

Gardens, 00–000; English, 00–000; English
   rococo, 000; English Tudor, 000; French, 00–000

Improvisations such as the following example have little to recommend them:

Gardens, 00–000; English 00–000;—rococo, 000;
  —Tudor, 000

Multiple indexes. Certain books require more than one index. Although the subject index ordinarily would include the material of such an index, the number and significance of the terms involved may make a separate index desirable. The indexes are described in the order in which they would be arranged following a subject index.

Contributor index: The names of the contributors to a multi-author work or symposium.

Author index: The names of the authors of works cited in the text (and often notes, references, and bibliography).

Title index: The titles of works cited in the text, usually in biography, literary criticism, and other critical works; the surname of the author appears in parentheses after the title. *Work* (author), 00.

First lines index: In anthologies of verse, songs, and other quotable matter, the first lines are often more useful to the searcher than the title.

Name index: The names of all persons of significance in the text, usually a work on biography, literature, history, or criticism.

Geographical name index: The names of all places of significance in the text, usually a work on geography, another earth science, or history.

Word index: An index of words and terms in a work in which significant concepts depend on their identification, such as a grammar, text on usage, or a work depending heavily on definitions and etymology.

Table of cases: In legal works a separate listing (similar to an index) made up of the court cases (decisions) cited. For a work in which case citations are few or of minor importance, the cases may be incorporated in the subject index.

Further discussion and examples of format are to be found in chapter 5, "Style," and chapter 6, "Production."

Once the design (production) requirements for an index have been satisfied—mainly with respect to space—the searcher is best served by an index that informs quickly and simply. When a mixed format seems to be building up as entries are being prepared, a second look at how the concepts are being handled may show unnecessary complexities are being introduced.

SUMMARY

The function of index format is to present on a typed page the keys (entries) that will unlock the content of a book for the user (researcher). Through the elements of the page design the indexer arranges the concepts (terms) in a pattern of cues to content. Although the subject of the work (discipline) is the most important factor in decisions about format, production requirements also have a role.

Essential features of an index format are entries in alphabetical order followed by page number keys. The format must also provide for modifications, sub-modifications, and cross-references. Variations occur with the need for inversions and the ordering of homographs. Organizing these format elements is the underlying structure: a line-by-line, paragraphed, or mixed pattern.

An ancillary decision with respect to format is the ordering of indexes supplementary to the subject index: name indexes, title indexes, word indexes, and table of cases for legal texts.

CHAPTER 4

ALPHABETIZATION AND ORDER

Filing index entries in alphabetical order is the end game, the final move after a series of manipulations required to arrange the elements of entry heads and modifications according to an accepted standard. The manipulations begin with entry head construction and are carried on and refined until the final ordering and filing alphabetically.

A condensed list of elements that need to be dealt with shows the range: particles, punctuation, abbreviations, prefixes, symbols, diacritical marks, and numbers. It also involves inversions, homographs, page number keys (for illustrations and tables), and chronology and series ordering. In addition, all manipulations have specific applications to categories of persons, places, and things.

Rules for the proper arrangement of the listed elements have, in general, been those of the American Library Association for bibliographic records. In 1980 the ALA revised the rules to make them computer compatible; at the same time the rules were greatly simplified.

The principal features of the revised rules are based on: the "file-as-is" principle, word-by-word alphabetization, ignoring punctuation for filing purposes, and eliminating persons, places, and things categories in filing.

For back-of-book indexing, particularly computer-assisted indexing the rules are generally accepted. For indexes compiled by non-automated means, many indexers continue to use the prior standards. For the most part the ALA revised rules have been incorporated in the recommendations here. The following is a summary list of rules useful in back-of-book indexing.

1. Applying the principle ''nothing files before something,'' all spaces and their equivalents (dashes, hyphens, diagonal slashes, and periods) are considered as nothing.

2. Modified letters and characters as used in non-English alphabets are treated like their plain equivalent in the English alphabet.
3. Punctuation and all non-alphabetic signs and symbols are ignored for filing purposes.
4. The ampersand (&) is filed as its spelled-out language equivalent (or ignored).
5. Abbreviations are arranged exactly as written.
6. A prefix that is part of the name of a person or place is treated as a separate word unless it is joined to the rest of the name directly or by an apostrophe without a space.

This chapter contains basic information on alphabetizing and order and also the principles for making choices among alternatives.

GENERAL METHODOLOGY AND TECHNIQUE

Being able to name the letters of the alphabet in order is only the beginning in index alphabetizing. In indexes an alphabetical arrangement is called for both *down* the page and *across* the type line.

The sorting of the slips (or cards) for arranging alphabetically may be seen as having four steps: (1) initial letter in heads, (2) sequence of letters in key words in heads, (3) initial letter in modifications (and sub-modifications), and (4) sequence of letters in modifications (and sub-modifications). (The publisher may request that the subheads be ordered by page number.) The size of the index determines the limits of each breakdown for first rough and then exact sorting.

Samplings of alphabetical works (for example, encyclopedias) have shown the distribution of letters to be about one-fourth each for A-C, for D-L, for M-R, and for S-Z. While the key terms and hence the alphabetical distribution are different for different subjects—a work on the Adams family would obviously give extra weight to the A-C's—this average distribution is a useful guide for a rough sorting of the entries in four groupings as a first step. When writing an index to space, this breakdown may be used to estimate how close the final index will be to the desired length.

After sorting by letter is finished, the breakdown may be

extended to the first two letters of the key terms for a large index or to the whole key term for a small index. A card file should be provided for roughly sorted entries; as needed, appropriate subdivisions of the alphabet (Ac, Al, Am, etc.) should be set up with file dividers. The final breakdown should be fine enough for the proper organization of homographs, the correlation of page numbers for duplicate heads and modifications, and the cleaning up of the index structure for final editing.

Preliminary rough alphabetizing *before all entries* are prepared precludes the efficient correction of error that often results from a change in text or folios (from author's alterations or production error). For each error to be found expeditiously, entries must be kept in the order of their preparation (by page number) until the entire text has been indexed.

The *groundwork* for alphabetization and order is laid as entries are prepared. The following section describes the basis for decisions that should be made as early as possible.

The index must reflect the text. This first principle in indexing is also the first principle in alphabetization. Problems arise when the text is inconsistent. Examples of such inconsistencies (in addition to spelling and terminology) are shortened forms (*Tintoretto* vs. *Il Tintoretto*), abbreviations (*USDA* vs. *United States Department of Agriculture*), and condensations (*steroids* vs. *corticosteroids*). Alternative terms may also be used (*tumor* vs. *neoplasm*). Such inconsistencies must be dealt with in index preparation if possible; if not, the task is an important one in alphabetization and order. An orderly index pattern is derived from a disorderly text by (1) choosing standard (preferred) terminology when inconsistencies arise, and (2) providing cross-references from the mutation to the preferred term.

The alphabetization scheme must be consistent. There are two alphabetization schemes to choose from: letter by letter and word by word. In the letter-by-letter scheme successive letters are alphabetized up to the punctuation that separates the *key term* of the entry head (or modification) from the page number(s), from a single modification, or from a similar separation in an inversion. All other marks of punctuation are ignored: apostrophe, hyphen, and comma in a series and also particles in certain instances (see subsequent discussion). In letter-by-letter alphabetizing the fact that a head (or modification) is made up of more than one word is ignored.

Applejack
Apple maggot
Apple pie
Apple-polish
Apple's farm

The word-by-word scheme has force *only* when the head (or modification) is a multiple-word term. The *first word* of the term determines the alphabetical order, secondary order being determined by the alphabetical order of the secondary term. (See also subsequent discussion of hyphens in compounds.)

Apple maggot
Apple pie
Apple-polish
Applejack
Apple's farm

The following section covers alphabetization puzzles that are not solved by knowing "how to alphabetize" by either of the described schemes; many of the principles are applicable only in the word-by-word scheme. (See also the subsequent section on order, for discussion of problems of inversion.)

PARTICLES: *Articles, prepositions, conjunctions.* In English an entry head introduced by an *article* (*a, an, the*) is a personal name, a geographic name, the title of an organization, the title of a work, or a first line. (See sections on persons and places.)

An article beginning the title of an organization is preferably dropped, *American Legion* (rather than *American Legion, The*).

An article beginning the title of a work is retained but ignored in filing: *A Tale of Two Cities.*

In an index of first lines (of verse or songs), a beginning article is retained and ignored in filing: *A Woman Waits for Me.*

An entry head introduced with a *preposition* is usually the title of a work or a first line. The preposition leads in all such instances: *In Memoriam; Out of the cradle endlessly rocking.* Another case is the anglicized name of a person with a prefix meaning *of* or *of the* (e.g., *de, van*). *De Kooning, Willem; Van Doren, Carl.* (For foreign names and how to deal with the space between the particle and the name, see section on persons.) A preposition or conjunction introducing a modification (or sub-modification) is ignored. The same is true of a preposition or prepositional phrase within the name of an organization, journal, and so on.

Antibiotics
   with analgesics
   for infection
   and sulfonamides (preferably *sulfonamides and*)
Journal of American History
Journal for Research in Mathematics Education
Association of American Publishers
Association for Asian Studies

An entry head introduced by a *conjunction* is again usually the title of a work or a first line, and it leads the entry: *When lilacs last in the dooryard bloomed: As You Like It.*

HYPHENATED ELEMENTS: *prefixes, compounds, unit modifiers, surnames.* In letter-by-letter alphabetizing, as noted earlier, hyphens are ignored. However, in the word-by-word scheme different uses of the hyphen call for different treatment.

Prefixes, hyphenated because of the doubling of a vowel (*pseudo-official*) or a combination with a capitalized word (*pre-Incan*), are treated as part of a single word.

Hyphenated *compounds* (except for unit modifiers, covered in the next section): Since the tendency in word formation is for open compounds and hyphenated compounds to be closed up, that is, to become one solid word (*hand book, hand-book, handbook*), such terms for purposes of index alphabetization are best treated as one word. In this same category are words hyphenated because of the doubling of vowels or the tripling of consonants (*bee-eater, shell-like*). Hyphenated *organization names* are treated as one word if incorporating a prefix (*Mid-South Company; Inter-American Defense Board*) and as two (or more) words if a created compound (*Johnston-Williams Company; Book-of-the-Month Club*).

Unit modifiers (compounds made up of two or more words to form a modifier) are treated as separate words: *second-class compartment, safe-deposit box, Ohio-Pennsylvania border.*

Surnames that are hyphenated (*Sainte-Beuve, Saint-Gaudens*), to follow the practice of *Webster's Biographical Dictionary* are best alphabetized as one word. (See also section on people.)

PUNCTUATION: *Comma (or other punctuation) in a series: apostrophe (as in a possessive); contraction of words, names, numbers; punctuation in titles, first lines, firm names.* In each of these situations the punctuation is ignored in alphabetizing. (See also hyphenated elements.) A possessive may also be converted to a noun modifier: *Farmers market, teachers college, child (for child's) behavior.*

Examples: *Vultures, hawks, and falcons; printer's devil; St. Peter's church; O'Malley; L'Enfant; Spirit of '76; Btu's; Dan'l (preferably Danl); Characteristics of Men, Manners, Opinions, Times; Beat! Beat! Drums!; Murphy's Music Store.* In all instances the punctuation is ignored.

ABBREVIATIONS: Abbreviations of *terms,* whether of two or more letters, initial letters, or acronyms, and whether closed up or used with a period following each letter, all are alphabetized as single units: *Corp., Bros., Mlle., Laser.*

U.S.
Usher
USSR

Abbreviations of *prefixes to proper names* are alphabetized as written (note exception in contraction of *L'Enfant* above). For example *M', Mc,* and *Mac; S., St.,* and *Ste.* However, unrevised style manuals retain the former rule of filling all forms under *Mac;* except for computer-assisted indexing, this ordering may still be used. (See also section on persons.)

SYMBOLS (see also section on scientific disciplines):

The *ampersand* is seldom used and may be alphabetized as if spelled out as *and (Saxon & Company. A & P, B & D).* It may also be ignored.

Mathematical codes (%, oz, HP) should be spelled out and so alphabetized.

Chemical symbols (Al for *aluminum,* S for *sulfur)* should be treated as if spelled out if retained. Almost without exception a chemical symbol can be spelled out. $c^{14}dating$ may be spelled out as *carbon-14 dating.* In either case it would be alphabetized as *carbon.*

DIACRITICAL MARKS. Diacritical marks are ignored. In the rare instance of homographs with and without diacritical marks (*resume* and *résumé*), the term with the diacritical mark would follow that without.

FOREIGN LANGUAGE CHARACTERS (mainly Greek, Scandinavian languages, Polish, German):

Greek characters are alphabetized as if spelled out, and if possible should be spelled out (*Alpha and omega; Phi Beta Kappa*). The scientific disciplines and mathematics present notable exceptions (see section on scientific disciplines).

In German the umlaut has orthographic equivalents: ä = ae; ö = oe; ü = ue. However, the umlauted vowel should be alphabetized as *a, o,* and *u.* That it has an orthographic equivalent (that is, *ae,* etc.) should be ignored.

Über der Rhine
Überweg, Friedrich

The Scandinavian languages and Polish are languages with expanded alphabets. The characters of these expanded alphabets are alphabetized as if the diacritical marks were not there. Any index that includes characters of an expanded alphabet should be preceded by an explanatory note on their use, particularly if those characters that expand the alphabet are placed at the end.

NUMBERS. How numbers are alphabetized depends on (1) whether the number is in the form of a figure or is spelled out, and (2) whether it is an ordinal, as opposed to a cardinal number, or occurs in a series. Numbers that are already spelled out are alphabetized according that spelling: Miscellaneous numbers are alphabetized as if spelled; *84 Charing Cross Road; 100 Days.* Dates are spelled as expressed and so alphabetized: *1982* would be "nineteen eighty two." The form for *100* "one hundred" and for *1,000* "one thousand."

Ordinal numbers (that is, numbers in a sequence), whether in figures or spelled out, are arranged according to the numerical order:

First Empire	Opus 101
Second Empire	Opus 106
Third Empire	Opus 111

Numbers in a series are arranged from small to large:

Congressional elections: 1892, 000; 1894, 000; 1910, 000

INVERSIONS. Alphabetization is affected by inversion, that is, bringing they key word forward, best demonstrated in the proper names of persons: *Smith, John.* The main indications for inversions are (1) proper names, (2) phrases with an adjective or noun modifier of key terms, and (3) table of cases. Inversions in modifications (and sub-modifications) are generally needless; the same result may be obtained by minor manipulation of the phrase. (For a full discussion of proper names of persons and proper names of places, see sections on persons and places.)

In phrases with an adjective or noun modifier of the key term, the object of inversion is to bring the key term forward: *Adjective, descriptive; Clause, subordinate; Sentence, compound.* In these and another example (given below), the phrase of the entry head may (and should) be considered a legitimate entry without inversion: *Descriptive adjective; Subordinate clause; Compound sentence.* When such an entry has modifications (and sub-modifications), two options are open to the indexer to reduce entries similar in content: (1) A cross-reference may be set up for the inverted head, or (2) inclusive page number *only* (no modifications) may be used to complete the inverted entry, and the modifications used to amplify the uninverted entry. This is proposed on the assumption that the researcher in the first instance is looking for the key term and in the second instance for the qualified phrase. The following example illustrates these options:

Without modifications:	Alcoholic hallucinations
	Hallucinations, alcoholic
With modifications:	Alcoholic hallucinations
	differential diagnosis
	treatment
	Hallucinations, alcoholic. *See*
	Alcoholic hallucinations
	or
	Alcoholic hallucinations
	differential diagnosis
	treatment
	Hallucinations
	alcoholic
	psychotic

Documents (treaties) and government organizations and publications should be subjected to inversion (or provided with an inverted cross-reference) when it is necessary to bring the distinguishing term forward: *Ghent, Treaty of; Observatory,* Smithsonian Astrophysical (also requires a cross-reference or uninverted head); *Public Printer, Annual Report of the.* But *Railroad Retirement Board; Food and Drug Administration; Constitution of the United States; Declaration of Independence, United States Department of State.*

In general, publications are best treated without inversion and with a cross-reference, if needed, from the key term: *Journal of the American Medical Association* (with cross-reference from the name of the association). Usually, a cross-reference is unnecessary: *American Journal of Psychology; Columbia Journal of World Business; Journal of Home Economics; Quarterly Review of Literature.* Newspapers are entered under the city of publication, whether or not it is on the masthead: *Los Angeles Times; Atlanta Constitution.*

In titles of works an introductory article is not inverted and is ignored: *The March of Folly; The Proud Tower.* Foreign titles are the exception, being filed as written: *Die Meistersinger von Nurnberg; Das Kapital.* In some instances the article may be omitted: *United States Government Manual.* In general titles are filed as written: *Leaves of Grass; Days of Wrath; Trial by Jury;* ''Body and Soul.''

Events, including conventions and expositions, may be best known by place, activity, or period: *Chicago World's Fair; Olympic Games; Centennial Exposition (Philadelphia).* Neither inversion nor cross-reference is indicated.

Organizations and institutions and buildings housing institutions are indexed under the official name with a cross-reference as needed to identify site or other description. No inversion is needed: *University of North Carolina; Museum of Science and Industry (Chicago)* with a cross-reference from *Chicago, Museum of Science and Industry.*

In a table of cases the citation is indexed under both names; and inversion is required in the entry for the defendant:

Roe v. Wade
Wade, Roe v.
Brown, Ex parte

Roe v. Wade, In re
Wade, Roe v., In re

ORDER

Alphabetization is only one of a number of devices used to organize the entries of an index. Others (in addition to inversion) are the order of (1) homographs, (2) page number keys, (3) entries in a chronology or series, and (4) subclasses of a major topic.

Homographs are words spelled alike but different in meaning. In subsequent sections each of these categories will be treated in detail. In general, identification of homographs must be self-evident or added. Note alphabetical order of identification

Lincoln, Abraham
Lincoln, Nebraska
Lincoln (breed of sheep)

Mercury (god)
Mercury (automobile)
Mercury (element)
Mercury (planet)

Medfield, Massachusetts: Seth Clark house
Medfield chest
Medfield (Mass.) joinery (key term is *Medfield joinery*)

The order of *page number keys* requires special treatment in an index that includes references to illustrations and tables when inclusive page numbers are involved. The question is: how should the page number keys be coded when an illustration (or table) falls *within* the succession of inclusive pages? A practicable solution is to place the italicized page number key to the illustration *after* the inclusive pages. (Table coded by *t*.)

Shaker furniture, 32–43, *47, 49,* 53t

If the illustrations cover the exact same pages as the text: Shaker furniture, *32–54*. If the illustration is only on the first or last of the inclusive pages: Shaker furniture, *32–54*; *or* Shaker furniture, 32–*54*. (See chapter 5 for alternative styles.)

Chronology or series. There are alternatives to the alphabetical arrangement of indexes. Some alternatives are mandatory, some expedient, some to be avoided. Arranging *modifications* in the order of occurrence in the text matter has sometimes been used in works of history and biography. Such an arrangement imitates outlining and assumes the user of the index knows the chronology of the events referred to.

A chronological or series order is indicated for index entries that are homographs, occur in a chronology, or represent a series. (See also section on persons.) The following examples cover the main situations for both entry heads and modifications:

William I (England)
William II (England)
William I (Prussia)
William II (Prussia)

World War I
World War II

Hague Peace Conference (1899)
Hague Peace Conference (1907)

Congressional elections: 1892, 000; 1894, 000; 1910, 000

Cranial nerves
    first (olfactory)
    second (optical)
    third (oculomotor)

Labor
    first stage
    second stage
    third stage
    fourth stage

A useful device, similar to that used for homographs, is the ordering of the *subclasses* of an extensively treated major topic to reduce and even eliminate sub-modifications and the typographical complications resulting. The following examples show several applications:

Diabetes mellitus (adult-onset)
Diabetes mellitus (juvenile-onset)

Leukemia (acute)
Leukemia (chronic)

Geometry (plane)
Geometry (solid)

Computer (analog)
Computer (digital)
Computer (hybrid)

Again, repeating the key term in successive modifications may be more meaningful than, and hence preferable to, setting up submodifications.

Legislature
  bills introduced,
  bills passed,

Another useful device is that for ordering *works,* not only of authors but also of anyone with a large output of titled productions. The main applications are in biography and history and criticism in the arts. The modification *works* comes at the end of the entry, where the titles are grouped together rather than being distributed among the other modifications.

Fokine, Michel, 000–000; . . . ; works: *Acis et Galatée,* 000; *Le Cygne,* 000; etc.
Brancusi, Constantin, 000; . . . ; works: *The Kiss,* 000; *Leda,* 000; etc.
Ravel, Maurice, 000; . . . ; works: *Boléro,* 000; *Daphnis et Chloé,* 000; etc.
Toller, Ernst, 000; . . . ; works: *Hinkemann,* 000; *Hoppla, Wir Leben,* 000; *Masse Mensch,* 000, etc.

The following sections on *persons, places,* and *things* cover some sticky details of alphabetization and order.

PERSONS

The main decisions affecting the alphabetization and order of personal names have to do with (1) homographs, (2) compound and hyphenated names, (3) changed and alternative names, (4) inversions, and (5) foreign names. The alphabetization of foreign names involves consideration of traditional usage, names with particles, and inversions.

An additional concern of the indexer is the complete and precise identification of persons inadequately identified in the text, the author (and editor) having assumed that the context makes the identification obvious. The indexer should provide the needed identification, preferably with the complete prename or two initials, if readily available, or query the entry on the index manuscript.

Homographs. Within the category of persons, homographs are arranged according to alphabetical order, chronological order, or numerical order in a series. Alphabetical order is determined by (1) prenames and/or initials, (2) occupation or other identification, and (3) nation or state of origin if needed for precise identification. As shown in the first example, initials always precede names beginning with the same letter.

Tate, H. C.
Tate, H. T.
Tate, Howard M.

Johnson, Samuel (clergyman)
Johnson, Samuel (lexicographer)
Johnson, Samuel (politician)

Smith, John (Kentucky legislator)
Smith, John (Louisiana legislator)

Chronological order of homographs is operative when dates or seniority is known.

Mason, William (1724–1797)
Mason, William (1829–1908)

Black, Robert M., Sr.
Black, Robert M., Jr.

Homographs are ordered numerically when the names occur in a series.

Elizabeth I
Elizabeth II
Pius VII
Pius VIII

Compound and hyphenated names. This category of personal names includes: (1) names with connective elements; (2) names of several parts, sometimes hyphenated; and (3) names that are appellations. The recommendations for alphabetizing are those of *Webster's Biographical Dictionary.* When in doubt, that work or the "Biographical Names" section of *Webster's New Collegiate Dictionary* should provide guidance. In addition to the examples given here, the section on foreign names covers the forms for specific languages.

Connective elements (particles) are found mainly in foreign names or names anglicized from foreign names and foreign names well established in English usage. The anglicized names and those well established are alphabetized under the particle.

Van Buren, Martin
Van de Graaff, Robert

De Forest, Lee
De Kruif, Paul
De Witt, Jan
de Soto, Hernando

Germanic names are alphabetized under the term following the particle.

Tirpitz, Alfred von
Schlieffen, count Alfred von
Marwitz, Georg von der

  Romance language names (except for those with articles such
as *la, le, les,*) are for the most part alphabetized under the term
following the particle. Alphabetization of those compounded with
articles depends on the weight of usage.

Castelnau, Michel de
Amade, Albert d'
Castro, Cristobol Vaca de
Cinq-Mars, Marquis de

But:

D'Annunzio, Gabriele
de Gaulle, Charles
La Fontaine, Jean de
Le Clerc, Jean
Argentina, La
Despenser, Hugh le
Ormesson, Le Fèvre d'

Names of several parts, sometimes hyphenated, are of several
sorts (in addition to those already covered under connective
elements): those with surnames made up of the union of names of
families jointed in marriage, and those that, for one reason or
another, are "created." This group also includes names compounded with *saint.*

Campbell-Bannerman, Sir Henry
Kingsford-Smith, Sir Charles Edward
Sackville-West, Victoria
Castro y Bellvís, Guillén
Ruiz Guiñazú, Enrique
Santa Ritta Durão, José, de
Saint-Exupéry, Antoine de
Saint-Gaudens, Augustus

Lloyd George, David
Vaughan Williams, Ralph
Fénelon, François de
    Salignac de la Mothe-

David Lloyd George changed his name from *David George;* the
name subsequently became hyphenated; however, the hyphen is
usually omitted. A cross-reference may be set up from *George,
David Lloyd.* See *Lloyd George, David.* The same practice should
be followed for other English compound names. For example,
Bannerman, Sir Henry Campbell-. See *Campbell-Bannerman, Sir
Henry.* In the case of *Fénelon,* the author may choose to use the
unhyphenated name alone; if so, the index would use the form
shown. It should be noted that the French are notoriously inconsistent in the hyphenation of both prenames and surnames.
    Appellations are names "given." Such appellations are treated
as surnames.

Carlos de Austria
Chrétien de Troyes
Catherine de Médicis
Crazy Horse
Henry of Blois
Enver Pasha
Joan of Arc
Peter the Hermit
Robert the Strong
Thomas à Kempis

Changed and alternative names. Perhaps the most common
name change is that of a woman when she marries. All women
have usage alternatives. A woman may take her husband's
prename as well as surname (Mrs. John Doe). She may retain her
own prename (Mrs. Mary Doe). She may retain her maiden name
(Mary Smith). She may combine her maiden name with her
husband's surname (Mary Smith-Doe). The following examples
show how such names may be organized as index entries,
depending, of course, on the emphasis in the text and the author's
preference.

Roosevelt, Mrs. Franklin (Anna Eleanor)
Roosevelt, Eleanor (Mrs. Franklin D.)
Roosevelt, Mrs. Franklin (née Roosevelt)
Gandhi, Indira (née Nehru)
Fontanne, Lynn (Mrs. Alfred Lunt)
Adams, Mrs. John (Abigail)
Adams, Abigail (née Smith)
Burney, Fanny (orig. Frances)
Burney, Fanny (Madame d'Arblay)
Bowen, Elizabeth Dorothea Cole (Mrs. Alan Cameron)
Curie, Irene (Madame Joliet-Curie)
Joliet-Curie, Irene (Madame Frédéric)

A large group of persons with changed and alternative names is made up of royalty and nobility, particularly British. The British royal family's official name of *Windsor* was changed in 1917 from *Wettin,* a German noble family. Similarly the title of a family of German counts, *Battenberg,* was renounced by English members for *Mountbatten.* An ascension to the peerage (in England to the rank of duke, marquis, earl, viscount, or baron) brings with it a title, amounting to another name. Titled persons are generally alphabetized under the title, not the family name, with appropriate cross-references. Exceptions are usually commoners who are elevated to the peerage in recognition of service.

Disraeli, Benjamin, 1st earl of Beaconsfield
Beaconsfield, 1st earl of. *See* Disraeli, Benjamin
Stewart, Robert, 1st duke of Albany. *See* Albany, 1st duke of
Albany, 1st duke of, Robert Stewart
Beaverbook, 1st baron, William Maxwell Aitken
Aitken, William Maxwell. *See* Beaverbrook, 1st baron

Pseudonyms, stage names, aliases, nicknames, and epithets, as assumed or given to writers, artists, actors, sports figures, and criminals, are alphabetized on the basis of a single principle: the name by which the person is best known. The following examples suggest the range. Cross-references are needed when precision is essential, as in biography, cultural history, or criticism; otherwise the main entry should be sufficient. *Always the author's usage should be followed for the main entry.*

Sand, George (pseud. of Amandine Aurore Lucie, baronne
    Dudevant [née Dupin])
Twain, Mark. *See* Clemens, Samuel Langhorne
Clemens, Samuel Langhorne (pseud. Mark Twain)
Villon, François (real name François de Montcorbier)
Boz, pseud. of Charles Dickens. *See* Dickens, Charles
Dickens, Charles (pseud. Boz)
Voltaire (pseud. of François Marie Aroute)
Boothe, Clare. *See* Luce, Clare
Luce, Clare (née Boothe)
Irving, Sir Henry (orig. name John Henry Brodribb)
Lawrence, Gertrude (orig. Gertrud Alexandra Dagmar Lawrence
    Klasen)
Bernhardt, Sarah (orig. Rosine Bernard)
Garbo, Greta (real surname Gustaffson)
Houdini, Harry (real name Ehrich Weiss)
El Greco (real name Domenico Teotocopulo)
Le Corbusier (pseud. of Charles Edouard Jeanneret)
Herblock (pseud. of Herbert Lawrence Block)
Lenin, Nikolai (real name Vladimir Ilich Ulyanov)
Ruth, George Herman (known as Babe)
Clay, Cassius. *See* Muhammad Ali
Muhammad Ali (given name Cassius Marcellus Clay)
The Cid (el Cid Campeador, real name Rodrigo Díaz de Bivar)
Calamity Jane (sobriquet of Martha Jane Burke)
Jack the Ripper
The Saint
Robin Hood

Personal names in modifications are troublesome only when the
full name is needed, as would be true in history or in biography
treating family members or persons with similar surnames. When
the full name must be given, it is alphabetized by the surname.

Account books: Edmund Bagge, 59–60; Martin Cockburn, 239;
    Hooe & Stone, 105; Jenifer & Hooe, 105; Ann Mason,
    78, 84–85; John Mercer, 68–72
Jefferson, Thomas: on federal city, 230, 231; George
    Mason IV and, 191, 208; John Mason and 249, 251;
    on Thomas Mason, 221

Inversion is a prominent feature in alphabetizing personal names, as has been shown in the previous sections. Some inversions of personal names are mandatory; others are a matter of usage; others depend on the form used by the author in the text. To summarize: (1) Prenames (and/or initials) are always inverted. (2) Particles introducing surnames may or may not be inverted. (3) Surnames of several parts are not inverted; cross-references from the second part may be required. (4) Appellations considered to be surnames are not inverted.

NON-ENGLISH PERSONAL NAMES

In addition to the principles on alphabetizing and ordering personal names covered in the previous sections, the indexer needs to have a handle on preferred usage, particularly of non-English names when the author's usage is ambiguous or nonstandard. Guidance on preferred usage is supplied by *Webster's Biographical Dictionary* and the ''Biographical Names'' section in *Webster's New Collegiate Dictionary,* already mentioned. Other sources are the various *Who's Whos, Facts on File, Keesing's,* and biographical dictionaries in specialized fields.

With population movements, particularly since World War II into the English-speaking countries, along with a communications revolution, foreign names in English publications have proliferated. Different alphabets (for example, Greek, Cyrillic, Hebrew, and Arabic) and ideogram systems (Chinese, Japanese) require transliteration (romanization); over time these transliterations are not consistent, although the Library of Congress transliteration system has promoted standardization in the United States. A common example of a difference in transliteration is that of the Russian *Tolstoi* or *Tolstoy.* The strong man of Libya is another: *Muammar Kaddafi* or *Muammar al-Qaddafi* (or *Gadafi*).

Decisions in this area should be those of the author or the editor, not the indexer. However, inconsistencies in the text often need to be resolved at the time of indexing, and the indexer, to save time, should have access to sources on current usage. Multiple-author and multivolume works are most likely to present problems.

Ancient names may also require judgment in choosing between

alternatives. Biblical and classical references may be particularly troublesome. The Jewish, Catholic, and Protestant Bibles use different names for the same person. The Greeks and the Romans had different names for the same deity. Roman rulers not only have different English variant names but also may have different names at different times.

Mark (Marc) Antony (Anthony) for Marcus Antonius
Augustus, original name Gaius Octavius, later Gaius Julius
Caesar Octavianus, sometimes Octavianus, English Octavian

Pompeius (English *Pompey*) may refer to four (or more) prominent Romans. Four Romans may also be referred to by *Brutus*. *Marcus Aurelius* may refer to two Romans, one also known as *Caracalla*. Whether a Roman name composed of a given name and surname (gens, or family, name) should be inverted is best determined by referring to a standard reference (*Webster's Biographical Dictionary*) and using a cross-reference if the author's usage differs.

Antonius, Marcus Aurelius
Marcus Aurelius. *See* Antonius, Marcus Aurelius

Non-English personal names may be roughly classified as European, African, and Asian, with further classification by language groups. Examples of some of the principles illustrated in the following sections have been given in previous sections.

Germanic languages: English, German, Dutch, Swedish, Norwegian, Danish:

Connective elements (particles)

Van Vechten, Carl (English)
Hoeppner, Ernst von (German)
Beethoven, Ludwig van (German)
Hoeven, Jan van der (Dutch)
                    but
Van't Hoff, Jacobus Hendricus (Dutch)
Klenau, Paul August von (Danish)

Names of several parts (sometimes hyphenated)

Armstrong-Jones, Anthony (English)
Bethmann-Hollweg, Theobald von (German)
Kamerlingh Onnes, Heike (Dutch)
Maurice of Nassau (Dutch)
Mies van der Rohe, Ludwig (German)
Paludan-Müller, Frederik (Danish)

Titles

Astor, viscountess, Nancy Langhorne Astor (English)
Derfflinger, baron Georg von (German)

Romance languages: French, Italian, Spanish, Portuguese, Rumanian:

Connective elements (particles)

Balzac, Honoré de (French)
Bernardin de Saint-Pierre, Jacques Henri (French)
Alarcón, Pedro Antonio de (Spanish)
Barros, João de (Portuguese)
Este, Beatrice d' (Italian)

Names of several parts (sometimes hyphenated)

Brillat-Savarin, Anthelme (French)
Batista y Zaldívar, Fulgencio (Spanish)
Alemán Valdés, Miguel (Spanish)
Blasco-Ibáñez, Vicente (Spanish)
Ugolini di Giacomo, Lorenzo (Italian)
Machado de Assiz, Joaquim Maria (Portuguese)

Titles

Montesquiou-Fezensac, comte Robert de (French)
Balbo, Cesare, conte di Vinadio (Italian)
Gondomar, count of. Diego Sarmiento de Acuña (Spanish)

Slavic languages: Russian, Polish, Czech, Serbo-Croatian, Bulgarian:

Alexander Nevski (Russian)
Rimski-Korsakov, Nikolai Andreevich (Russian)
Kropotkin, prince Pëtr Alekseevich (Russian)
Kaden-Bandrowski, Juliusz (Polish)
Krasínski, count Zygmunt (Polish)
Kolowrat-Liebsteinsky, count Franz Anton (Czech)
Kukulijevic-Sakcinski, Ivan (Serbo-Croatian)

Other Indo-European languages:

Brian Boramha (Gaelic)
Zeuxis (Greek)
Eusebius of Dorylaeum (Greek)
Kazantzakis, Nikos (Greek)
Dakki, Abu Mansur (Persian)

Finno-Ugric languages: Hungarian, Finnish, Estonian, Lettish, Lithuanian

Hevesy, Georg von (Hungarian)
Zichy zu Zich und Vásonykeö, count Géza (Hungarian)

Note: In Hungarian the surname always precedes the given name, thus *Hevesyi Beorg* (*von* replacing the *i* in English usage).

Semitic languages: Arabic, Hebrew, Turkic

In Hebrew, names with particles (for example, *ben* meaning *son*) and compound names are not inverted. In Arabic traditional usage the given name is followed by the family name or the father's and family name. In modern usage the family name comes first. Particles that are forms of *the* (*al-*etc.) preceding the name are not inverted.
Titles (*bey, pasha,* etc.) follow the name in traditional usage.

Ben-Gurion, David (Hebrew)
Bar Levi, General Chaim (Hebrew)

Har-Zion, Meir (Hebrew)
al-Wazir, Khalil (alphabetized under *W*) (Arabic)
Ibn Saud (Arabic)
Glubb Pasha (Arabic)
Abd-al-Malik (Arabic)
Sayigh, Sheikh Abdul Hamid (Arabic)
Hamid, Sultan Abdul (Arabic)
Kamal Bey, orig. Mehmed Namik (Turkic)
Mehemet Ali (Turkic)
Ziya Gõk Alp (Turkic)

 Asian personal names. Personal names in the countries of Asia
and Indonesia have both traditional and modern usage modes in a
number of language groups.

Indo-Chinese: Chinese, Thai (Siamese), Burmese:

 In Chinese the surname comes first, followed by the given
name(s) in traditional usage. In modern (Westernized) usage the
surname is last and is inverted in alphabetization. In Thailand and
Laos (Lao being a Thai language) the given name precedes the
family name and is usually inverted, although usage may vary
with the author. In Burmese the given name(s) only is used,
preceded by a title (Dr.) or term of respect (U).

Mao Tse-tung (Chinese)
Tao-tzu (Chinese)
Chang Hsüeh-liang (Chinese)
Kung, H. H. (Chinese)
Kittikachorn, Thanom (Thai)
Panomyong, Pridi (known as Mr. [Nai] Pridi) (Thai)
Le, General Kong (known as General Kong) (Lao)
Phouma, Prince Souvanna (Lao)
Thant, U (Burmese)
Ne Win, General (Burmese)

Khmer (Cambodian official language), Korean, Japanese, Vietnamese:

 These distinctive languages have the surname first followed by

the given name(s). In westernized usage the order is reversed, and
the surname is inverted. In Vietnamese and Cambodian tradition,
as in other southeast Asian countries, celebrities are addressed by
their personal name and title.

Pho Proeung (westernized Pho, Proeung) (Khmer)
Norodom Sikhanouk (westernized Norodom, Sikhanouk)
   (Khmer)
Rhee Syngman (westernized Rhee, Syngman) (Korean)
Park Chung Hee (westernized Park, Chung Hee) (Korean)
Okuma Sigenobu (westernized Okuma, Shigenobu) (Japanese)
Kamimura Hikonojo (westernized Kamimura, Hikonojo) (Japa-
   nese)
Nguyen Cao Ky (known as Marshall Ky) (Vietnamese)
Ngo Dinh Diem (known as President Diem) (Vietnamese)

Indic and Dravidian language groups are the main languages of
the Indian subcontinent and Sri Lanka (Ceylon): In India, Hindi,
Marathi, and Bihari dialects; in Bangladesh, Bengali; in Punjab,
Panjabi of the Indic language group. In India, Telugu and in Sri
Lanka Tamil of the Dravidian language group. Modes for alphabetizing personal names are complicated by titles, religious and
honorific (Islamict and Sikh), and caste and clan names. The
following examples show the principle modes. In general, alphabetization in modern usage is determined by the surname, which
may be an honorific or be followed by an honorific. Many historic
names are treated as surnames of several parts, often including an
honorific (for example, *ali, khan, shah*).

Nehru, Motilal
Gandhi, Mohandas Karamchand
Ghose, Sri Aurobindo (*Sri*, title of respect)
Maghunath Rao (*Rao*, caste name)
Ranjit Singh (*Singh,* Sikh designation)
Mitra, Rajendralala
Jafar Ali Khan
Ali Vardi Khan
Siraj-ud-daula

In Indonesia most of the many spoken languages belong to the

Malayo-Polynesian language family; Bahasa Indonesia is the national language. Traditionally Indonesians are known by a single name, sometimes supplemented with an Islamic honorific.

Suharto
Hatta
Nasution, Abdul

African personal names. There is no clear correspondence between African national boundaries, tribal definition, language groups, and usage with respect to personal names. Main language groups are Semitic, Hamitic, Bantu (mainly Kafir, Zulu, and Swahili), and Hausa in north and central Africa. In South Africa the official languages are English and Afrikaans (Cape Dutch). The languages of the colonial powers have persisted despite the independence movements and also affect the order and alphabetization of personal names, westernization being the current mode in Western language publications. African tribal names carry the surname first in traditional usage.

Hamani Diori (tribal order)
M'ba, Leon (alphabetized as *Mba*)
Amin, Idi
Obote, Milton
Tubman, William Vacanarat Shadrach
De Wet, Christiaan Rudolph (Afrikaans)

PLACES

Problems with alphabetizing and ordering place names occur mainly with homographs and names of several parts. Where a place is identified by both ancient and modern names or by names in several languages, which name should be the main entry and which the cross-reference(s)? Guides to ordering place names are *Webster's New Geographical Dictionary,* the "Geographical Names" section in *Webster's New Collegiate Dictionary, Rand-McNally Atlas,* and *Columbia Lippincott Gazetteer of the World.*
   Homographs. [Categorization of place names that are homographs is indicated only for references such as gazetteers.] Two

principles determine the arrangement of the homographs: alphabetical position of limiting geographic entities and administrative importance. Places in the United States may precede those in other countries in alphabetical order, or all homographs may be ordered alphabetically according to country, administrative unit (state, province, county, city, or town), and physical feature. The examples show the alternatives.

United States precedence	*Alphabetical order*
Victoria (Ill.)	*Victoria (Argentina)*
Victoria (Kans.)	*Victoria (state Australia)*
Victoria (co. Tex.)	*Victoria (British Columbia)*
Victoria (Tex.)	*Victoria (Chile)*
Victoria (Argentina)	*Victoria (Ill.)*
Victoria (state Australia)	*Victoria (Kans.)*
Victoria (British Columbia)	*Victoria (co. Tex.)*
Victoria (Chile)	*Victoria (Tex.)*
Victoria (river, Australia)	*Victoria (river Australia)*
Victoria Lake (Africa)	*Victoria Lake (Africa)*
Victoria Lake (Que.)	*Victoria Lake (Que.)*

Names of several parts. Such place names are alphabetized the same as other multipart terms according to the chosen scheme (word by word or letter by letter). They are subject to inversion only when the first element is thought of as descriptive: *Erie, Lake; Ranier, Mount; Fear, Cape; Malvinas, Islas.* But *Mount Desert Island.* When the term has the sense of an epithet, it may not be inverted: *Bay of Pigs, Cape of Good Hope. Webster's New Geographical Dictionary* does not make this distinction, and it may be wise to follow *Webster's.* Place names abbreviated in the text are alphabetized as if spelled out. The examples show the main forms for ordering place names of several parts.

Al Bab, Syria
Da Lat, S. Viet.
De Soto, Kans.
Del Mar Beach, N.C.
Den Burg, Neth.
Des Lacs, N. Dak.

El Salvador, Chile
Le Havre, France
Les Cayes, Haiti
Los Muermos, Chili
Plains, The, Va.
Sainte-Anne, Guad.
Saint Anne, Ill.
Saint Jacques, N.B., Can.
Saint-Jacques, Que,. Can.
The Everglades
The Narrows

When a place name as part of a head has only descriptive significance, it is treated as a "thing," not as a place. In alphabetizing, parenthetical identification is ignored.

Raleigh, Sir Walter
Raleigh, N.C.
Raleigh (N.C.) Memorial Auditorium

Changed, alternative, and foreign-language equivalents for place names. The primary guide to decision-making is to follow the author's usage for the main index entry head and supplement it with cross-references as needed. For example, a text on the ancient history of the Middle East would refer to modern *Istanbul* as *Byzantium.* A text on the Ottoman Empire would refer to it as *Constantinople.* Current history would refer to the city as *Istanbul.* In the first two instances, a cross-reference from *Istanbul* would be appropriate. Modern *Ethiopia* was formerly *Abyssinia;* only in very precise historic definition would a cross-reference be necessary from *Abyssinia.*

The handling of foreign-language equivalents for place names in current usage depends on the author's preference and the readership. *Falkland Islands* would be sufficient identification for British readers; *Islas Malvinas* (inverted) would be an appropriate cross-reference for a non-Commonwealth audience.

In general, foreign-language equivalents as cross-references to place names again depend on the context. In English publications, English is the choice for the main entry head. The indexer should be alert to audience expectations in relation to the author's usage in the text. The following examples illustrate equivalents that might require cross-references, particularly in translations.

English	*Foreign language equivalent*
Belgrade	Beograd
Cologne	Köln
The Hague	Den Haag, or 's Gravenhage
Florence	Firenze

THINGS

Synonyms (and the validity of cross-references from alternative terms); abbreviations, acronyms, and symbols; and homographs (their identification and ordering): these are the areas of general concern in alphabetizing *things*.

Synonyms have to be anticipated, recognized, classified, and sometimes supplied. Synonyms should be anticipated in disciplines that are on the frontiers in science and technology. Recognizing synonyms depends both on knowing the vocabulary of the discipline and on being alert to clues in text context, illustrations, and tables. Synonyms are classified as *preferred* (for main entry head) and *alternative* (for cross-references); the term for the main entry head should be selected early and stayed with, the alternative(s) for the cross-reference(s) being selected as the indexing progresses. When an author uses nonstandard terminology, the indexer should supply the alternatives (as cross-references) that the searcher would expect to find.

Abbreviations and acronyms. For abbreviations and acronyms the shortened form should be supplemented with the term in full whenever (1) the context is new, (2) the text is didactic, or (3) the usage is ambiguous. The question is, which—the shortened form or the full term—should be the main entry head (supplemented with the alternative form in parentheses), and which the cross-reference, if needed. Abbreviations and acronyms are so common in scientific and technical literature that the full exposition of the term may be more confusing than the shortened form. The following abbreviations and acronyms are best entered as the main entry head, the full form in parentheses being optional:

AFL-CIO, AIDS, CIA, Conrail, DDT, Laser, SALT. Whether an abbreviation or acronym, with or without periods, the term should be alphabetized as a single unit.

Homographs. Terms spelled the same but with different meanings are more likely to turn up when indexing the names of persons and places than when indexing things. In homographs of things the parenthetical identification should be both precise and consistent. Homographs needing identification are more common in encyclopedic works than in specialized texts. The example, admittedly strained, illustrates the point:

House (architecture) *not* (building)
House (astrology) *not* (zodiac)
House (commerce) *not* (firm)
House (government) *not* (legislature)
House (zoology) *not* (bird)

The following sections deal with problems of alphabetization and order in different disciplines.

Scientific text. The terminology of science places certain restraints on alphabetization and order. In addition to the common occurrence of synonyms (and the need for cross-references), neologisms, abbreviations, acronyms, and symbols, scientific text is full of multiterm concepts. In scientific terminology, such multiterm concepts are expressed as compounds or phrases, often based on Latin precedents: for example, structures in anatomy, scientific names in biology, diseases in medicine, compounds in chemistry, and celestial bodies in anatomy. In alphabetizing, such compounds or phrases must be presented in full and in normal order (not inverted). The following examples show a correct arrangement.

Ursus horribilis
Magnolia acuminata (not M. acuminata)
  grandiflora
  virginiana
Choroid plexus
Golgi apparatus
Endoplasmic reticulum
Pemphigus vulgaris
Adenosine triphosphate

Calcium chloride
Ursa Major
Nepheline syenite
Quartz diorite

Symbols. Greek letters function as symbols in chemistry (β-amylase), medicine (β-*hemolytic streptococcus*), astronomy (δ-Aquilae), and statistics (β-level). (Note that the letter following a *retained* Greek letter is capped if the index style calls for entry heads to be introduced with a capital: β-Amylase.) When a Greek letter is retained, it is ignored. When it is spelled out, it is alphabetized as spelled. Isotope symbols leading an entry head should be expressed in full and alphabetized as spelled out. Chemical expressions for compounds should also be expanded and alphabetized as spelled out. The following examples show the treatment of such expressions.

^{128}I *becomes Iodine 128*
$_pO_2$*measurement* becomes *Oxygen tension measurement*

Certain expressions (such as *pH* referring to *hydrogen ion concentration*) are not directly expandable and should be alphabetized as a unit (often in a cross-reference).

Some symbolic expressions in chemical formulas (*p-aminobenzoic acid*) are alphabetized as spelled out (*para-aminobenzoic acid*) if the symbol is retained.

Still other symbolic expressions are ignored in alphabetizing:

D-Threonine
L-Threonine
l-Alanine
d-Alanine
cis-Dichlorethylene

Humanities text. An indexer of text in the humanities faces multiple decisions about both alphabetization and order. The names of artists and works often include particles. (See sections on "Particles" and "Persons.") Titles may include punctuation. Titles may also include modifying terms that need to be ordered. The following examples cover the most commonly encountered entry patterns:

ARCHITECTURE
    Trinity Episcopal Church, Roslyn, Long Island
    Tryon's Palace, New Bern, North Carolina
    Renaissance revival style
    Renaissance style
    Fenestration: Harbor Hill, 00; Tuckahoe, 00
    Façade: Boston Public Library, 00; Harbor Hill, 00

LITERATURE
(Titles of works are indexed under both the title itself and the
author's name. An exception would be a work on a single author,
where title entries would suffice.)

Fielding, Henry, 00–000; works: *Tom Jones,* 00; *Tom Thumb,* 00;
    Tumble-Down Dick, 00
Tom Jones (Fielding)
Pound, Ezra, 00–000; works: *Cantos,* I-XVI, 000;
    Exultations, 00; "Greek Epigram," 00; *Ripostes,* 00
"Long I thought that knowledge" (Whitman)
"Long, too long America" (Whitman) (Punctuation ignored)

MUSIC

"Non so d'onde viene," aria (Mozart)
Cosi fan tutte, opera (Mozart)
Piano concerto no. 1, C major (Beethoven)
String quartet, G major (Mozart)
Symphony no. 4, G major (Mahler)
Petrouchka (Stravinsky)

PLASTIC ARTS

Caricature and cartoon
    Apologies for Tippling (Charles)
    Between Two Stools (Charles)

Painting
    Isabella Stewart Gardner (Sargent)
    Benjamin Franklin . . . (West)

Sculpture
  David, Florence Academy (Michelangelo)
  David, Casa Buonarroti, Florence (Michelangelo)
  Pietà, St. Peter's Rome (Michelangelo)
  Pieta, Rondanini Palace, Rome (Michelangelo)

Social science text. Despite the diversity of the disciplines subsumed under the category *social sciences* (mainly, political science, economics, sociology, psychology, law, anthropology, and religion), to the indexer they present common problems: they are loaded with theories and concepts. They are grounded in institutions and organizations and events. Documents (historical, political, legal, and religious) are often the research material for workers in these fields. Attention to a single principle of entry organization will simplify decision making: *Avoid inversions.* Setting up cross-references in instances of possible uncertainty on the part of the researcher provides additional insurance. Multiterm concepts and the names of institutions and documents are *not* inverted in the mind of the index user. Thus, never *cost of living* under *living; Declaration of Independence* under *Independence;* or *Oedipus complex* under *complex.* The principal need for cross-references is with the names of organizations and government departments when the name contains a prepositional phrase. (For government departments and agencies, see index to *The United States Government Manual.*) *American Medical Association* needs no cross-reference. However, one would be useful for *American College of Surgeons* under *Surgeons, American College of.* The same would be true for *National Institutes of Health.* Tables of cases may include inversions.
  The following examples show the construction of entries most likely to be generated in the social sciences.

Theories and concepts

Manifest destiny
Gunboat diplomacy
Keynesian theory
Balance of payments
Factors of production

(Note: This concept would also be entered under *production* as
a *modification: Production, factors of.*)
Child behavior
Death wish
Father image
Civil rights
City planning

Institutions and organizations and events

Age of Reason
Battle of the Bulge
War of 1812
Council of Trent
Immaculate Conception
Sacred College of Cardinals
Protestant Episcopal Church
European Economic Community
American Library Association
Chamber of Commerce
United Mine Workers
American Airlines
Merrill Lynch, Pierce, Fenner & Smith

Documents

Declaration of Independence
Versailles Treaty (but Ghent, treaty of)
Apostles' Creed
Constitution of the United States
Employment Act (1946)
Ezekial (Douay Bible, Ezechiel)

Table of cases (law)

People v. Mistriel
Mistriel, People v.
Brown, Ex parte
Raines v. State, In re
State, Raines v., In re

Moody Co., J.H., U.S. v.
J.H. Moody Co. U.S. v.
U.S. v. P.N. Jones Co.

SUMMARY

The information presented in this chapter may seem to amount to a lot. However, applying most of the rules becomes automatic as the indexer gains experience. Moreover, if the indexer is aware of the existence of rules governing symbols, numbers, abbreviations, and diacritical marks and looks them up when necessary, there is nothing unmanageable in the ordering and filing of index entries for back-of-book indexes.

Here, as elsewhere in the methodology and technique of indexing, the principal concern is the satisfaction of the user. This goal is attainable by attending to consistency: in alphabetization according to the chosen scheme (word by word), in the use of preferred terminology with appropriate cross-references, and in the use of concept organization recognized as standard for the index user's discipline.

CHAPTER 5

STYLE

No piece of printed matter is without "style," since all style has to do with type, not only as distinguished by different fonts (type size, face, weight, etc.) but also as the source (font) for the characters used in spelling, capitalization, hyphenation, numbers, and symbols.

Two facts about style are significant. Style has a base in tradition, as a consequence of which there are essentially few variations between "style books." Second, style without *consistency* is no style at all. For it is the factor of consistency that makes possible the identification of usages as being "style."

Index style, along with index format (which to a certain extent determines style details), presents the index to the index user, and its importance outweighs the importance of text style. No line in an index is without an obvious style point.

Competent consistent styling makes possible instant recognition of the index message. To achieve this objective, styling begins with index entry preparation as the entry heads and modifications are composed to fit a predetermined model (line by line, paragraphed, or combined). Styling is continued through alphabetization and ordering and is refined in index editing, when only a minimum of additional styling should be necessary. Styling should *not* be put off until later.

The responsibility for thorough styling rests squarely with the indexer. The in-house index editor should not have to clean up an index's style.

This chapter is organized by specific style features, in order: capitalization, format, illustrations and tables, cross references, distinctive features, and page numbers.

Index style encompasses typographical preferences—*beyond those* for the text—for: capitalization, punctuation, abbreviations, symbols, numbers, cross-references, and format mark-up. Styling also involves editing, mainly to tighten copy and ensure correct use of particles (prepositions and conjunctions).

In keeping with the publisher's requirements, the style must provide for inclusive pages, illustrations and tables, notes, volume numbers (for multivolume works), and sometimes such signals as *et seq., f., ff.,* and *passim.* Any index with signals for special material (such as illustrations) should be preceded by an explanatory note, for example: Page numbers in *italics* refer to figures; page numbers followed by *t* refer to tables.

Although entries should be styled as they are written up, the style sometimes needs to be modified as the indexing progresses, particularly when the terminology is in conflict with what is possible with the publisher's composition technology.

A first principle in index style is quick visual recognition of entry heads, modifications, and cross-references. (As noted earlier, style consistency should *not* be confused with the syntactical requirements of the text, which are not relevant to index construction.) Each format pattern (entry a line, paragraphed, or combined) has distinct requirements with complementary styles. The possible combinations are detailed in the following sections.

CAPITALIZATION

Entry head and modifications. Some styles call for an entry head to be introduced with a capital letter; others opt for lower case (proper terms, of course, being capitalized). With the drive toward simplification with the advent of computer-assisted indexing, lower case gained support. On the other hand, for back-of-book indexes with audiences used to more traditional styles, the enhanced visual recognition from the *contrast* between capitals to introduce entry heads and lower case for modifications has much to recommend it.

Shrimp	shrimp
creamed,	creamed,
curried,	curried,
with dill,	with dill,
Louisiana style,	Louisiana style,

Syrup	syrup
caramel,	caramel,
chocolate,	chocolate,

On the other hand, entry heads in a *list of terms* are best introduced with lower-case letters.

The practice of capitalizing all nouns in modifications has nothing to recommend it; it is seldom found in present-day publications.

Cross-references. See section on styling cross-references.

Symbols. Chemical terms preceded by a symbol are capitalized: b-Carotene, cis-Dichlorethylene. Note the term *pH*; as an entry head it retains the same form as in the text.

PUNCTUATION

The format—line by line, paragraphed, or combined—determines punctuation style.

Line-by-line. There are basically two line-by-line formats that affect punctuation; the difference is whether or not the entry head is followed by page numbers

In the first instance a comma is placed between the head and page number(s), between the terms of an inversion, and between successive page references. In modifications (and sub-modifications) followed by page numbers, a comma is placed between the key term and page numbers and between successive page numbers. (Recall that there is little if any reason for inversions in modifications)

English gardens, 225–232, 426, 453
   history, 226–227, 427
Scott, Mary, 425–426

In the second instance (where the entry head is *not* followed by page numbers), two styles are to be recommended; a third (sometimes used to save space) tends to confuse the researcher. In one recommended style the head (whether or not an inversion) stands alone. In the other recommended style the head is followed by a colon. The same style is used for modifications.

    English gardens
       history, 226–227, 427
       landscape architecture, 325–327
    Scott, Mary
       birth, 426
       marriage, 430

    English gardens;
       history, 226–227, 427
       landscape architecture, 325–327
    Scott, Mary:
       birth, 426
       marriage, 430

    English gardens, 225–226
       history (or: history:)
          16th century, 230
          17th century, 231

The third (not recommended style) places the first modification on the same line as the entry head, subsequent modifications being placed on separate lines.

    English gardens, history, 226–227, 427
       landscape architecture, 325–327

When an entry head is followed by a single modification (not to be confused with an inversion), the modification is on the same line as the head.

    English gardens, history, 226–227, 427

Here the ambiguity found in the previous example does not exist. (See also section on styling cross-references.)

Paragraphed. For an entry head followed only by page numbers and with only one modification, the style is the same as that for entry-a-line format.

English gardens, 225, 232, 426, 453
   English gardens, history, 226–227, 427

For an entry head followed by page numbers and a succession of modifications, the style differs only in that the successive modifications are followed by semicolons.

English gardens, 225, 232, 426, 453; history, 226–227, 427; landscape architecture, 325–327

An entry head *without* page references is followed by a colon.

English gardens: history, 226–227, 427; landscape architecture, 325–327

A useful style feature of the paragraphed format is the grouping of works at the end of an entry (rather than distributing them alphabetically), the term *works* being followed by a colon.

Fielding, Henry, 196–324; birth, 196; education, 200–216; as playwright, 294–313; works: *The Modern Husband,* 300; *The Temple Beau,* 302; *Tom Jones,* 311

Combined (mixed; modified). In the line-by-line format, the only difference is in handling sub-modifications: The modifications are arranged line by line, and the sub-modifications are run in with semicolons between successive sub-modifications.

English gardens, 225–232, 426, 453
   history, 226–237, 427; 16th century, 230; 17th century, 231

In the paragraphed format, modifications preceded by an em dash are arranged line by line and followed by sub-modifications separated by semicolons. A modification without a page number preceding a sub-modification is followed by a colon.

English gardens, 225–232
   —history, 226–227; 16th century, 230; 17th century, 231
   —landscape architecture, 325–327; Jefferson on, 328

—plant catalogues: American collections, 415; English collections, 417

(See also section on styling cross-references.)

ILLUSTRATIONS AND TABLES

Publishers have various styles for coding index references to illustrations (figures) and tables. Details of the coding should be given in an introductory note. For example:

Page numbers followed by the superscript ^{r} refer to reproductions. Or: Page numbers in *italics* refer to figures.

A common device is to italicize the number of a page with an illustration. Another is to precede the number with (*illus.*). For works in the fine arts the number may be followed by the superscript ^{r} (standing for reproduction).

English sparrow, 46–*49* or perhaps 46–48, *49*
English sparrow, 46–48, (illus.) 49
Balzac (Rodin), 659^r

For tables the code following the page number is *t*. Or (*table*) preceding the number. For a map the code would be (*map*).

CROSS-REFERENCES

Format determines the location of cross-references, both internal and external, and in turn, style preferences. (See chapter 3 for the appropriate patterns.) Style for cross-references is mainly a matter of capitalization versus lower case and the use of italics, parentheses, and periods.

The prime signal for an external cross-reference (from an entry head to an exact equivalent) is the word *See* in capitalized italics. That for an internal cross-reference (from the entry at hand to some subdivision of the entry content) is *See also,* again in capitalized italics. For the entry-a-line format no punctuation follows the cross-reference. The index entry referred to is styled in roman.

Garden design. *See* Landscape architecture
Gardens, 425–527. *See also* Landscape architecture
    American, 498–502
    English, 503–517

(See chapter 3 for other locations for internal cross-references in an entry-a-line format with modifications.)

In the paragraphed format with modifications, the internal cross-reference is placed at the end of the entry without terminal punctuation.

English gardens, 225–232; history, 226–227; landscape
    architecture, 325–327. *See also specific landscape*
    architects

While the foregoing style points represent the dominant current practice, different publishers may call for a number of variations. The indexer needs to study the publisher's house style with care to avoid styling error.

Note that for any cross-reference to a work that is italicized, the *see* and *see also* are in roman.

Girl of the Golden West. See *La Fanciulla del West*

Internal cross-references from the head or modifications in the paragraphed format are difficult to handle. The following example shows the styling, with lower case to introduce the reference and parentheses for enclosure:

English gardens, 225–232 (*see also specific sites*);
    history, 226–227; landscape architecture, 325–327;
    plantings, 340–350 (*see also* Plant catalogues)

DISTINCTIVE TREATMENT

From time to time an index may turn up details that require distinctive styling.

Notes. An index reference to a note must be keyed if the matter

in the note is *not* an amplification of matter in the text. They key
(n) may (or may not) be italicized and followed by a period (*n.*).

English gardens, 185, 189n (or 189*n.*)

End notes (those at the end of a chapter or the book) should
include the number of the note:

English gardens, 189n (205)

Symbols. A term preceded by a symbol is capitalized (if that is
the index style for entry heads). A prefix to a term (often
italicized) follows the style of the text.

β-Carotene,
cis-Dichlorethylene,

Abbreviations. Such abbreviations as *&* and *Co.* are permitted
in an index while prohibited in text. For any extensive use of
abbreviations, an explanatory note should precede the index.

Major emphasis. An index may need to differentiate discussions of major and minor importance. Page numbers may be
printed in bold face (or italics) to indicate such emphasis. A note
at the beginning of the index should state what the style is. (If
italics are used for emphasis, they obviously should *not* also be
used to key illustrations.)

English gardens, **225–236,** 465, 515

An index entry on an author may include reference to quoted
material. Such a reference may be keyed by *quoted* in parentheses.

Jefferson, Thomas, on English gardens (quoted), 314

PAGE NUMBERS

Page numbers may require styling for (1) inclusive numbers, (2)
parts and multivolume works, including series and cumulative
indexes, and (3) a decimal classification system.

Inclusive numbers. A condensed (abbreviated) style for inclusive page numbers is not always to be preferred. The rationale that the system reflects "the way we *say* continued numbers" overlooks the obvious: that such numbers are read, not said. Also, how much is saved in character count in an average index with the condensed system is not easily calculated. The system, in brief, for styling an index is:

Under 101: 2–10, 91–100, 100–104
101 and 1001 and over (except 1000 and other amounts
ending in zeros): 101–4, 307–14, 391–425, 1004–7, 1021–24,
  1121–22
But 1000–10024

Indefinite page references. Today indefinite page references, once fairly common, are seldom used and are not to be recommended. The signals are:

f., ff.	and following page (pages)	425f., 425ff.
et. seq.	and the following	324 et seq.
passim	here and there	525–590 passim

Parts and multivolume works. Page references in indexes to works comprised of parts and to multivolume works, including series and cumulative publications, must include a key to the part, volume, series, and so on. The following examples cover style considerations:

Volumes 3:249–260 or 3:249–260
Parts in volumes pt. 4, 3:249–260
Volume with parts vol. 3, pt. 4:249–260
Series
    By year '55:102
    By month with volume marker 3:249–260 (Ja. '55)

(Abbreviations for months are: Ja, F, Mr, Ap, My, Je, Jl, Ag, S, O, N, D.)

Decimal classification system. When a text is organized by numbered sections within chapters, the index may be keyed by chapter:section number and often with page numbers as well. The chapter number introduces the key, followed by the section or sections.

English gardens, 2.55–57

TABLE OF CASES

In legal works, whatever the style for case citations in the text, case citations in the index or a separate table of cases should be styled in roman.

Abbot v. Andrew, In re
U.S. v. Hamilton

SUMMARY

The difference between a well-styled index and one that is not is obvious, even to those who are not familiar with what "styling" means. The appearance of an index page that is effectively styled has a look of authority. A poorly styled index, despite the quality of the index entry content and organization, raises a question about the soundness of the index.

The indexer can go far toward achieving the objective of a consistently styled index by styling entries thoroughly, insofar as possible, at each step in the indexing process. By this means the need for cleaning up index style in the final checking and editing will be minimal.

The responsibility for a well-styled index is that of the indexer and should not be passed on to the in-house index editor.

CHAPTER 6

PRODUCTION

The one variable in the production of an index is the manuscript; everything else, as will be explained, is fixed within a limited range: type style, type size, column length and width, number of columns per page, and number of book pages available for the index. The manuscript is an ''unknown'' that must be fitted into the frame of the type and page design and space. Furthermore the production of the index—marking the index manuscript up for composition and makeup—is not only the last item on the index designer's agenda but also close to the last item on the production staff's agenda for the book. Put these facts together and it becomes obvious that a well-prepared index manuscript of satisfactory length, suitable for the text subject matter, and formatted in a pattern consistent with the publisher's style is most to be desired. Nothing is less welcome than an index manuscript that is excessively long or short or of inappropriate or inconsistent format. With foresight, the distress of a bad index manuscript can be avoided.

Left to his/her own devices an inexperienced indexer—particularly an author-indexer—may choose an inappropriate model for a back-of-book index. An inappropriate model, for example, would be the index format for a yearbook, one which uses the left-hand column for entries and the right-hand column for page number keys, with leaders from the entries to the page numbers. The manuscript of such an index requires considerable work by the in-house editorial staff.

An index that is excessively long or short is a similar burden on the in-house production staff, which must fit the copy into the available space. An excessively long index may also require considerable editorial revision if it is accepted despite the flaw.

These crises can be avoided by foresight in the selection and instruction of the indexer, that is, by dealing with an indexer whom the publisher knows to be experienced. If the designated indexer is the author or a new freelancer, all basic information about index style and format and the desired index length should be provided, along with a sample proof to show what the index should look like.

The more an indexer knows about book design and production in general and index production in particular, the better equipped the indexer is to cooperate with the in-house editorial and production staffs. This chapter covers the essentials.

There are two phases to index production: that before copy preparation and that after index manuscript is received by the production staff. In the first phase—before copy preparation—the basics of index format are laid out along with the basics of book format. The basic minimums are page size and type style. Maximum specifications would cover type size, column length and width (translated into character count per line), format (line by line or paragraphed), and total index pages.

These decisions about index design may be exclusively those of production or may contain some editorial input. For example, editorial may ask for an index length and pattern suitable for the text at hand. With this information and a castoff of the manuscript, production is able to project the number of pages (lines) available for the index consistent with the book format.

In the first instance, with the only production specifications being page size and type style, index format and length are left up to editorial and the indexer, perhaps with editorial advice about the number of index items per text page. With an experienced indexer this alternative produces a satisfactory result in most instances. However, after the book has been made up, production may find it has too few or too many pages left over for the index. If too few pages are available, type size may be reduced and columns lengthened. Cutting copy should be a last resort: a good index has an internal integrity, and arbitrary deletions may considerably decrease its value. If too many pages are left over, the best solution is to end the book with blank pages (perhaps headed ''Notes''). It is practically impossible to ''blow up'' an index after the manuscript is completed. Also, extensive leading and shortening type lines give the impression of a debased product. Another suspect device is to thin out a paragraphed index by converting some entries to a line-by-line pattern.

With maximum specifications for an index, the indexer makes all the ''adjustments.'' There is no index that cannot be written to space, modifications of text concepts being either amplified or contracted. However, the specifications an indexer receives may be so inappropriate for the text at hand that it would be folly to follow them. The cause may be communications failure between production and editorial, or production decisions made without editorial input. The indexer should present the case for altering the index specifications before beginning work or as soon as the difficulty becomes apparent.

As has been pointed out, production decisions for an index are largely the production decisions for the book, *specific* index specifications being either fixed before manuscript preparation with the manuscript to be written to space, or put off until the manuscript is received. With a manuscript written to space, production tasks to prepare the edited copy for composition are minimal: checking for aberrations that would alter total line count (critical only if the runover would require a change in the size of the last signature) and marking up copy for typesetting. (See following sections.)

If the manuscript has *not* been written to space, the first production task is to find out how close the copy comes to filling the space set aside for the index, consistent with the projected type size and column width and length. The line count for the manuscript is compared with the line count for the space available for the index. If the result is reasonably close, the manuscript may be marked up for typesetting. If the manuscript is long, the runover may be taken care of by increasing the column length (or width), or by reducing the type size. The easiest solution is to increase column length enough to get the needed additional lines. Increasing column width involves reducing margins and the space between the columns; the gain will be in characters and is not easy to compute. Since an index is usually set in 8- or 9-point type (with a point of leading) and the space between columns is 1 pica, not much is gained by this solution unless the index is quite long. (It should be noted that with the flexibility of photocomposition in terms of type face and size and spacing, a number of manipulations may be used to make an index "fit," unless it is excessively long.) If the manuscript is too short, the columns may be shortened or the type size enlarged. (See former comment about alternatives.) Space may also be added between alphabetical breaks.

DESIGN AND ESTIMATING

The typeface for an index is the same as that for the text. A standard type size is 8 or 9 point with 1 point leading (8/9 or 9/10). The index may also be set solid (without leading). For a tight index the type size may be 7 or even 6 point unleaded. Leading of 2 or 3 points may also be added if the index needs to be lengthened.

While two columns per page is the usual design for an index, a three- or even four-column page may be used for a book of large dimensions. For standard book sizes, an index column of 50 lines (giving 100 lines per page) is common. For a book of large dimensions, the column may run 10 to 15 lines longer. Space between columns may range from 9 to 12 points (1 pica).

Estimating index length has two aspects: (1) projecting length for the indexer, and (2) estimating for composition. In the first instance the estimate is a guesstimate. Certain factors may be critical. How dense is the text, that is, how many names and technical terms need to be indexed? How repetitious is the text? Index *items* in index preparation are not the equivalent of index *entries* in the finished manuscript. A repetitious text will result in multiple page references for heads and modifications. Another factor is whether heads and modifications are going to be made up of single- or multiple-word terms. Multiple-word terms will raise the percentage of turnovers (lines that run over onto the next line). (Obviously, in index written to space will reduce the consequences of a bad guesstimate.)

For a start, one page of index should be provided for every 50 pages of uncomplicated text. Depending on text density, the number of index pages may be increased to one for every 30 pages of text. In terms of index *items* per page (or column for a two-column text page), the range from uncomplicated or dense text would be from two to three items to five to seven. In terms of turnovers, 25 percent of the space estimate should, on an average, be assigned to that use. For example, assuming one page of index for every 50 pages of an uncomplicated text of 400 one-column pages, eight pages would be projected for the index. At 100 lines per page (50 lines per column), the total would be 800 lines, reduced to 600 if 25 percent is set aside for turnovers. Assuming three index *items* per page, the total would be 1,200. With two page references per head or modification in the finished manuscript, the copy should fit the space projected. Obviously, good editorial input is essential for accurate space projecting. Note that, since the estimating is done in terms of *lines* as representing heads, modifications, and turnovers, the method will work for both the line-by-line and paragraphed index pattern, the paragraphed form being the more elastic.

Estimating for composition is necessary when the index manuscript has been prepared without definite instructions as to design and length. The purpose is to find out whether the copy received will fit the space available, in terms of the typeface and size desired. The first step is to make a line count of the copy, that is, of heads and modifications. This number of lines converted into pages (at 100 lines per page, for example) plus 25 percent turnovers will be the number of pages needed for the index. If too much or too little, adjustments may be made in column length, type size, leading, or column width, as previously discussed. In all calculations about space for an index, the estimator has the sinkage at the beginning of the index and space between letters of the alphabet to manipulate.

MARK-UP FOR COMPOSITION

Directions for index composition are marked up on the copy and also included in covering memorandum (a composition order). If index copy includes signals for special typography (such as for illustrations), these must also be explained. The following list is an example of such specifications. (See also chapter 3, "Format.")

Column width - 13 picas; ragged right
Columns per page - 2
Lines per column - 50

Typeface - Times Roman
Type size - 8/9
Indentation
    Entry head - flush left; turnover 2 em
    Modification - 1 em; turnover 2 em
    Sub-modification - 2 em; turnover 2 em
Last page - 6 lines minimum
Continued lines - repeat head with (*continued*)
Running heads - verso; book title or *Index*; recto: *Index*
Space between letters - 2 lines; with initial letters, 2
    spaces above, 1 space below

In addition to the foregoing, the job must be identified by book title and author. The book page on which the index begins must also be included.

PROOF

Time for handling index page proof in the publishing house may be as little as one day. Neither the author nor the indexer sees the proof. (The author may or may not have seen the index manuscript; if an inexperienced author tries to evaluate an index manuscript, the result may be nitpicking and serious loss of time.)

In the publishing house, editorial checks index proof for flagrant content error and typos; production checks for deviations from the desired index design. Electronic manuscript including computer-assisted indexes calls for additional procedures in getting the manuscript ready for production. (See chapter 10, "Computer-assisted Indexing.")

SUMMARY

In index production the index manuscript is the "unknown" element. All other elements are "known" within an adjustable limits.

1. Book length determines index length in terms of pages: what is left over in the last signature (a printed sheet of

pages folded to comprise an eight-, sixteen-, or thirty-two page unit).

2. Book type determines index type style.
3. Index type size is within a limited range, 8 or 9 pt.
4. Number of index columns per page is within a limited range: 2 or 4.
5. Number of index lines per column is within a limited range: 50 more or less.
6. Index *format* (line by line or paragraphed) and index *length* are determined by the index manuscript submitted by the indexer.

When it is possible to make adjustments within the listed limits so that the index copy will fit the available space, production of an index is routine. However, (1) if the indexer submits a manuscript patterned after an inappropriate model; (2) if the manuscript is excessively long or short for the subject and text length; or (3) if the designer's guesstimate is off the mark, adjustments are difficult. The short manuscript, if acceptable in other respects, may be saved by a number of manipulations of type size, leading, and spacing. An excessively long manuscript has a good chance of being rejected; if accepted and subjected to in-house editorial revision, the production of the book will likely be delayed.

Such misadventures may be prevented by foresight in negotiations with the indexer; credentials should be carefully examined, and a sample of the indexer's work should be requested. Both the untested freelance indexer and the author-indexer should receive specific instructions about the publisher's requirements with respect to estimating index items per text page, format, and style, plus a proof of a publisher's index as a model.

While the indexer is not a direct participant in the planning or execution of the index design, the work of the in-house staff is affected by what the indexer submits in the form of a manuscript. The professional indexer is obliged to be knowledgeable about book production in general and index production in particular.

CHAPTER 7

REVISIONS

Not every book has a potential for revision. Some books are sure to be revised, and others will never be revised. In the first category are yearbooks, encyclopedias, and loose-leaf publications, all of which undergo revision on a regular basis. Also in this group are elementary- and high-school textbooks, which are generally revised in-house.

In the second group are books that never get beyond the first edition, ''dead'' history and biography, and profitable books on the publisher's back list, whose facts never change and that are continually reprinted without revision.

In between are factual books subjected to revision at intervals because new facts convince the publisher that a ''new and revised'' edition would increase sales. The last mentioned are of some interest to the freelance indexer, although it is more likely that the index will be revised in-house rather than being contracted out. However, with the proof method, it is possible for the freelance indexer to undertake the revision.

In planning ahead for a revision of a book in the third category it would be well for the publisher to let the indexer know of his or her expectations. Since the basic objective of a revision is to get the obsolete material out and the new material in, anticipating obsolescence in planning main entry heads can reduce the detail of an index revision. The key is to differentiate between solid information of lasting importance and ''instant'' history, events of transient interest, and fleeting popularity.

Information of passing significance may be effectively subsumed as modifications under entry heads. The scheme of main entry heads in the *World Almanac* (1992) is instructive. The almanac publisher's focus is on the *world,* the basic organization of entry heads being by country (nation), permanent institutions (such as those of the United States government), and recurring events. Persons are regarded as ephemeral. To have your name as a main entry, you have to be a "world shaker," and/or "notorious," and preferably dead. For example, *Mikhail Gorbachev* and *Boris Yeltsin, H.R. Haldeman,* and *Spiro T. Agnew* have entries. *Nelson Mandela* and *Walter Mondale* do not. Otherwise names of persons are subsumed under countries (places) or events as *participants* in *events. Margaret Thatcher* appears under *United Kingdom; Einstein* appears under *Atomic energy.* Also *Persian Gulf War* but no *Norman Schwarzkopf.* The thrust of the yearbook's organization is according to broad categories of enduring facts made current by modifications on details.

Admittedly, a yearbook pattern cannot be copied for a back-of-book index, the subject of this manual. However, attention to setting up enduring concepts for the main entry heads, with supporting and possibly transient details in the modifications, is applicable to any back-of-book index, particularly one that is likely to be revised.

Of importance in index revision is cost. Is starting from scratch going to cost less (in terms of time as well as money) than patching up an old index? Critical factors are: the type of publication, the extent of the revision, the index pattern, and whether the previous index was prepared with a revision in mind.

As noted above, books of facts and statistics reissued annually (yearbooks) or continually updated (encyclopedias) or loose-leaf publications, and having a fairly rigid assembly of heads, are proper candidates. In such works the pattern is fixed; only statistics and supporting details are changed from year to year and edition to edition; deletions and additions are mainly of subentries in entry heads.

A revision of a back-of-book index is less chancy if the changes are few, spotty, and mainly a matter of updating, or are in blocks of sections or whole chapters, than if many text pages are affected. If the previous index was prepared with a revision in mind and the index copy (such as on cards) was saved, the revision process is routine. If not, and the index revision is to be prepared with page proof from the previous edition, the revision is complicated but possible.

The choice between a revision and a new index for a revised text may depend on who is going to do the work. For yearbooks and encyclopedias, there is usually continuity in the index staff along with standing materials (card or computer file) and procedures for index revision. Such continuity is unusual when the original index was prepared by the author or a freelance indexer. An author should not be expected to have the know-how to prepare an index revision. The freelancer who wrote the original index may not be available to prepare a revision. And since indexers vary in the approach to "thinking" an index, few indexers will willingly revise an index written by someone else. A viable alternative is for the index to be revised in-house; any index editor should be able to handle a routine revision.

Another matter related to an index for a revised text is the expectation that the indexer will approach the task in the same way as the original indexer and that the original index should be used as a guide. Trying to analyze and absorb the previous indexer's approach and justify that indexer's decisions can only be compared with unscrambling an egg. However, the index to the previous edition will give the indexer of the revision an overview of the text coverage.

For a spot revision to succeed, the format and folios must (with minor exceptions) remain unchanged. Such an index revision is concerned not only with deletion of references to deleted text and addition of references to new material, but also with any movement of text between pages.

Essential materials for an index revision are: (1) proof of the standing composition of the previous edition with changed lines clearly marked, (2) proof of the pages reset, and (3) proof of the previous index. The indexer should carefully compare the old and the revised proofs for error in the changes marked: makeup error, particularly between pages; and miscellaneous error in the revised text, as in spelling.

To summarize, the tasks of an index revision are: (1) deletion of references to materials omitted from the current revision; (2) addition of entries to new text material; and (3) copy preparation on cards or manuscript for composition.

The following sections detail the procedures for revision of an index with cards or proof.

REVISION WITH CARDS

How the revised index is to be composed, whether entirely reset or partially reset with revisions fitted into standing composition (on film), affects the revision method with cards. In the first instance, the object is to prepare the entire alphabetized card file for composition. In the second instance, it is to get spot revision copy keyed onto proof of the previous index for composition and film patching.

To get an overview of what the index revision will involve, proof of old and revised text pages should be compared. It is useful to mark off the areas of change on the revised text proof and tick significant terms.

The following step-by-step procedure is used when an index on cards is to be entirely reset.

1. The cards are refiled by page number (1, 2, etc.). Cards for cross-references should be refiled in a separate section.
2. Cards are checked against revised text proof, and cards for entries (and modifications) no longer valid are deleted. If a card has keys to a subsequent text page(s), the card is moved forward to the next page reference. The card is destroyed if all page references are deleted.
3. New index cards are made up for new text material, edited, styled to conform to the standing index pattern, and filed by page number. A running count should be kept of cards deleted and new cards filed.
4. The entire card file index is realphabetized and in the process checked for stylistic consistency.
5. The cross-reference file is checked against the newly realphabetized index file for verification or correction. The cross-reference cards are then realphabetized.

A final step is to compare the count of cards deleted with those added to find out whether the index has been overly expanded or contracted. This estimate should be sent to production along with the index card file.

When an index on cards is to be used in a spot revision on standing composition (film), the following procedure is followed.

1. The cards are refiled by page number.
2. Cards are checked against revised text proof, and entries (and modifications) no longer valid are deleted. These cards are pulled and placed in a separate file. When this checking procedure is finished, the cards in this set-aside file are checked for additional deletions in subsequent text pages. These cards, as marked for correction, will be the basis for *deletions* on standing composition.
3. New index cards are prepared for new material in the revised text proof and set aside, as were the deleted index cards.
4. Cards in the "set-aside" files are compared with index proof from the previous edition. The proof is corrected for deletions, and new copy is prepared for new entries and attached to the proof. After final editing and styling, the revised proof is ready for production.
5. Cards representing deletions are destroyed. Cards representing new entries are inserted into the standing index file. Since this file is not going to be used for composition, it need not be realphabetized.

Note: Numbering the cards in an alphabetized index file is a time-saver when the file has to be realphabetized. Deletions or additions with a revision are easily indicated.

INDEX REVISION WITH PROOF

Using index proof from the previous edition may be indicated when the text needs to be revised to (1) correct a flagrant error, (2) include an important discovery or event, or (3) include an additional or extensively revised chapter or part.

The task has three parts: (1) deleting index references to text material that has been eliminated, (2) adding index copy for new text material, and (3) marking up the revised index proof for production (editing, styling, cross-reference checking, etc.).

Getting rid of no-longer-valid index entries call for concentration and a sharp eye. With a set of revised text pages (marked for areas of change) and proof (or copyprint) of the index from the previous edition, the index is scanned for *page numbers* involved in the text revision. All invalid page numbers are deleted, while the key entry terms are retained. These same changed text areas are then indexed (on cards or slips) and the entries alphabetized. This file of alphabetized additions is then checked against the proof of the previous edition, corrections are made, and copy for new material is attached. (By mounting the old index proof on a sheet of paper, room will be provided in the margins for corrections and new copy). Standing index entries are deleted when all page numbers have been deleted on the proof and no new page numbers have turned up; new page numbers are added to index entries still valid. In addition to copy for new entries, copy may be needed for entries that have to be reconstructed because of the incorporation of new material. As a final step, the mounted index proof is edited and styled for delivery to composition. Cross-references are also checked for validity.

Composition of the revised index copy may require resetting blocks of type beyond the areas of correction. Here meticulous proofreading is a must, as it is when an index revised on proof is entirely reset.

SUMMARY

For yearbooks, encyclopedias, and looseleaf publications, revision is routine and ongoing by a permanent staff of indexers. Main entry heads, for the most part, are "fixed," deletions and additions being in modifications, not in standing entry heads.

Revision of a back-of-book index for a nonfiction trade book is also likely to be carried out in the publishing house, although with the proof method, the revision may be successfully assigned to a freelance indexer.

Anticipating the likelihood of the need for a revised edition will simplify index revision if the original indexer has this possibility in mind. If a revision is likely, the original index should *not* be prepared by the author, but by an experienced indexer well known to the publisher. In setting up the original pattern, the indexer can aim at establishing main entry heads that will endure and not likely be subject to change.

CHAPTER 8

SPECIALTIES

Experience has made it clear to me that the more one knows about how a book came to be, the better equipped one is to cut through to the essentials in indexing. Hence in this chapter we shall look at the goals of authors and publishers, how these goals are reached, and possible impediments that the indexer would do well to know about.

Almost all books that require indexes are on so-called specialty subjects. In fact, this book in its entirety treats the various aspects of specialty indexing that apply to the large discipline groupings: science and technology, humanities, and social science. Another group is included because of its importance in publishing: textbooks and reference works.

A word about indexer qualifications for specialty indexing: technical skill is practically useless unless the indexer is well grounded in the terminology of the discipline. Since it takes time to get a good hold on specialty terminology, an important prerequisite for the indexer is basic education in the germinal fields. The indexer should also own up-to-date references in the area of specialization, at a minimum a dictionary and some basic texts.

SCIENCE AND TECHNOLOGY

The importance of publications in science and technology is shown both by the size of this arm of the publishing business and by the impact of science on economic and social policy. As of today, seven percent of the US national economy is just one facet—the health care business. And if we look at the observable components of this one application of science—medicine and its related services (e.g., pharmacy, nursing, medical technology, and hospital management) and the related manufacturing and business enterprises (pharmaceuticals, appliances, and diagnostic and therapeutic equipment)—it is but one step to the fact of the need for masses of published information.

Regardless of the field of science involved—whether the basic sciences (physics, chemistry, and biology) or one of the innumerable splinter groups (e.g., biochemistry, physiology, biophysics), or one of the applied sciences of which medicine along with related health services is but one—the purpose of all publications in science is to satisfy the need for facts.

The source of facts in science is scientific research. And both the methods of conducting and reporting that research are reflected in the organization and content of scientific publications and in turn in the work of an indexer. The process of scientific research is slow and deals with minutiae. A single research project may involve years of repetition of a single experiment, one tiny detail of the experiment being tested time after time to observe any change in results. Equipment and materials and testing conditions all may influence the outcome. The expenditure of time and the cost of equipment make publishing results, even negative results, imperative in order to continue to get funds to support the research. However, the goal of the researcher is to be able to publish progress (positive results) on some aspect of the research problem ahead of competing colleagues. Competing colleagues, on the other hand, turn to such publications in order to compare methods and results with their own work.

The main channels for presenting the results of original scientific research are in periodicals (such as *Nature, Science,* or the *New England Journal of Medicine*) and in papers read at scientific meetings (later collected for publication in book form). From these original publications the research findings are widely disseminated in yearbooks or in annuals of professional societies, in monographs (which may cover the research on a single project over many years), in books on applications of the research, and in textbooks. In every secondary publication, the essential data of the original report are supplied in a reference: author, title, publication, and date. Such references are an important feature in the indexing of scientific publications.

The described connection between the original research report and the far reaches of a textbook point to the importance of the organization (format) of the original report, which in fact is widely used in publications throughout the scientific community. The findings (data) from the research project, obtained by individual experiments, are tabulated; summaries of these tabulations are then worked up for presentation in tables, graphs, and charts. Only then does the researcher begin to think about the manuscript that is to be the vehicle for disseminating the report through publication.

The essentials of a research report are: a hypothesis, a tentative assumption based on a synthesis of prior observations and theory; a description of the research project as designed and carried out to test that hypothesis; and the results of the research. For a research report for a journal, the pattern, often carried over to contributions to symposiums on a specific topic, includes a succinct statement of the design of and the results of the research; an introduction stating the problem, methods, and goals of research; the body of the report consisting of a description of the research materials and methods used in measurement and analysis; data from such measurements and analysis; and a conclusion or summary. With some modifications and simplifications, downstream scientific publications follow the same general pattern. To identify these manuscript divisions and other divisions of the text, centerheads and sideheads are used, the tables and graphs are provided with headlines (captions). Illustrations may be included with legends detailing their content and significance.

To the indexer the foregoing description of scientific research and the preparation of research results for publication has special importance: The most reliable source of concepts for entries is in the graphic display of data—tables, charts, graphs, and illustrations. Furthermore, the most reliable terminology preferences are also to be found in graphic data. And as was emphasized in the discussions of methodology (chapter 1) and technique (chapter 2), other sources of entry material are to be found in the heads to text divisions, a prominent feature of scientific publications.

Because of the importance of references in scientific publications, the names of the authors of the cited works—appearing in the body of the text as well as in the references—are often listed in a separate index. These references, unless the book is relatively short, usually appear at the end of each chapter or section with a reference number (locator) with the author's name in the text as a code to the citation (Brown[3]). Because inconsistencies between names in the text and those in the references are often found to be pervasive, the index of author names should be prepared before the body of the text is indexed.

A list is made up of the complete names in the order in which they appear in the section of references. This list is compared with the same name in the text, the spelling is confirmed if possible (and is otherwise questioned), and the page number of the text citation is added to the names on the list made up from the reference section. Errors are sent to the publisher for correction in the text or in the reference section.

The line-by-line pattern is to be preferred for indexes in the sciences. A single term in science may be heavy with meaning, and visual access to it needs to be quick and unequivocal. The line-by-line pattern with the vertical alphabetical arrangement of terms and concepts is better designed to fill that need than the paragraphed pattern.

The terminology of the sciences affects not only the indexer's approach to the material but also index style. Styling details may involve a range of type manipulations. For example: caps and italics for taxonomy (*Ursus horribilis*); Greek letters in chemistry, physics, mathematics, and astronomy; small caps in chemistry (D-glucose); numbers of radioisotopes (iodine-131). Symbols (Al for aluminum) and abbreviations (VHF) and acronyms (AIDS) are also common. When scientific text calls for index references to tables and illustrations, the use of bold face for emphasis in an index may be required. Alphabetization is also affected by the occurrence of prefixes in scientific terms (*cis*-dichlorethylene).

Since many terms and concepts in science are legitimate compounds and phrases, the temptation to form inversions should be scrupulously avoided. Also to be resisted is any impulse toward outlining.

Problems may turn up with multiple-author works: contributors may use different terminology, and the terms used may not be those preferred by the discipline. An example is the terminology for drugs and scientific equipment. With respect to drugs, an appropriate standard is that the generic or chemical designation is preferred, followed by the proprietary name (trademark) in parentheses. A cross-reference from the proprietary name(s) is indicated if it is used as an alternative in the text. New equipment, particularly if the research is concerned with its use, should be indexed under the trade name, as well as under any generic designation. For standard equipment, the generic name is enough.

HUMANITIES

It is hard to find a unifying focus or definable goals in any of the disciplines comprising the humanities, goals such as one finds in science and technology. Because of these definable goals, scientific publications have both structured organization of content and a structured text format. It is this structure that gives the indexer of such books valuable orienting guides. Such orienting guides are not a standard feature in the humanities.

Considering the diversity of subject matter of the humanities, absence of a unifying defining focus is to be expected. But even within a single discipline no compelling ambition or economic motivation drives authors and publishers to seek a consensus with respect to goals.

The humanities, broadly defined, have in common a cultural character. Originally, the term applied only to polite scholarship—Greek and Latin classics (philosophers, dramatists, poets, historians, etc.). Today a broad classification would include the fine arts (architecture, music, painting, sculpture and other plastic arts); literature, particularly criticism; history (the course of human events) and biography (the history of persons).

However, despite this diversity these disciplines have a common characteristic that is a useful orienting guide in indexing: the substantial number of concepts that are proper names—people, places, events, objects (works), documents. Persons have attributes (birth, education, achievement, etc.) and connections with other people, events, places, and things, which also have attributes and connections. Here we have the relationships that are material for modifications. It is interesting that in index structure (head-modification relation), persons have precedence over places, and persons and places over things. *Places* as well as *persons* are legitimate entry heads in their own right, as well as in a modifying relationship with persons. For example, the Michelangelo-Rome relationship would be

Michelangelo	*not*	Rome
at Rome		Michelangelo at

or   Michelangelo-*David* relationship

Michelangelo	not	David
David		Michelangelo

also	*David*	(identification of creator
	(Michelangelo)	of work *not* a modification)

Because of the plethora of names in the humanities, the question of what to include and what to leave out of the index should be faced at the outset; in essence, this means what proper names may be left out. Is the name *significant* or merely incidental in the context. In history and biography in particular it is not enough for a person to be only an observer of an event, or a place to be only a name on an itinerary, or an event to be only a calendar day (Christmas), or a work to be on the biographee's reading list. The name must have significance both as an entry and as a modification.

A major feature of books in the humanities is material on an artist's or writer's work. In a book on a single artist or writer, a separate index on works is useful with an index entry on the title as well. For a book on a number of artists or writers, the works are listed at the end of the index entry on the artist or writer, as well as in a separate entry:

Fielding, Henry, xxx; modification, xxx; modification, xxx; works—*Joseph Andrews,* xxx; *Jonathan Wild,* xxx; *Tom Jones,* xxx; *Amelia,* xxx

A separate index of all the works discussed in the text is also useful.

Books on criticism and theory are undoubtedly the most

difficult for the indexer to deal with. Authors of such books are likely to tackle the index themselves, feeling unsure about the ability of anyone else to do the work justice. Such authors are also most likely to complain about an indexer's work. The concepts are often multiterm and obscure and have special meaning for the initiate. Some help may be found in terms used in references and bibliography: titles of books or periodical articles help validate the form for the terms in the text.

Although indexes in the humanities may be built on a line-by-line pattern, the paragraphed form is generally to be preferred. The horizontal distribution of modifications conserves space without loss of visibility, and may even improve the grasp of relationships between key terms. Also sub-modifications are rarely if ever needed.

While the usage in the index is governed by the usage in the text, the indexer may find multiple inconsistencies in spelling, the styling of works, English versus foreign-language equivalents, and facts in text versus legends for illustrations. The occurrence of inconsistencies needs to be called to the attention of the publisher.

Also setting up cross-references to preferred terms from alternative uses may require fine judgments. Problems of alphabetization and order are not uncommon, for example, in names with particles or when a name refers to more than one person, work, or institution. In dealing with styling inconsistencies, it is safe to opt for the preferences of the *Chicago Manual of Style.*

Various perspectives on a topic are implicit in a work in the humanities, that is, the who, the what, the where, and the when. Moreover, the *what* perspective implies classification. The index user may begin his or her search for any one of these views, depending on his or her primary need. For example, the researcher may have in mind any one of the key terms in the following sentence: "The potential relationship between the thrust of Shaftesbury's moral philosophy and the more abstruse elements of Burlingtonian architectural theory . . . has not been sufficiently analyzed." Using the index methodology principle of "isolate and recombine," the indexer would come up with these entry heads and modifications:

Shaftesbury, Anthony Ashley Cooper, influence on Burlingtonians

Moral philosophy, influence on Burlingtonian theory
Burlingtonians, architectural theory
Architectural theory, Burlingtonian

When a major work requires separate indexes, for example of names, titles, or terms, each index should be prepared separately, the subject index being worked up last.

SOCIAL SCIENCES

As is true of the scientific disciplines, the principle disciplines grouped under the rubric of social science have commonalities useful to the indexer. These disciplines study human's behavior as a social animal: his or her group and institutional relationships (sociology); his or her behavior as a producer and consumer of goods (economics); his or her mental processes in relation to behavior (psychology); his or her relationships with political authority (political science, law); his or her beliefs and behavior in relation to the supernatural (religion); his or her origin, distribution, and classification (anthropology).

As science seeks explanations for natural (physical) phenomena through observation and instrumentation (physical) measurement to test a hypothesis (theory), so social science uses observation, testing, and measurement to support theory. However, while there is a great body of data (''facts'') about the physical world that are accepted as ''true'' by the entire scientific community at a given time, there are no *nonhuman* (physical) instruments to test and measure human behavior; in the social sciences both the observer and the observed are human. As a consequence, in the social science community there is no consensus about what is ''true.'' Also, in the absence of an objective (nonperson) measure of the results of testing, the social sciences rely heavily on quantities (statistics); much of social science research is in the accumulation of massive amounts of data. Furthermore, in the absence of a consensus, conflicting theories about human behavior give rise to ''schools,'' each with its own set of principles to explain the phenomena. Hence, neomalthusian, Marxist, Ricardian, Keynesian, and neoclassical schools in economics; Freudian, neoFreudian, Adlerian, and behaviorist schools in psychology.

Common methods of research in the social sciences are interviews and reports of cases (examples of human social interaction in a specific situation or a controlled environment). "Numbers" from surveys, such as those conducted by government agencies, are subjected to statistical analysis to test their validity. Publications reporting such research depend on graphic displays as a starting point in presenting the results. The main purpose of such research publications is to add to the fund of knowledge about human social behavior. At the same time, there is a group of works in the social science disciplines whose sole purpose is to advance a theoretical position or support a "school." (Many of these books, fortunately, are not thought to need an index.)

What does all this mean to the indexer faced with a social science text? First, research reports in the social sciences that present results in graphic form are usually well organized, and, as in the physical sciences, this organization provides concepts for index entries. Second, other useful clues come from the fact that social man has attributes; these provide a basis for statistical analysis and hence material for graphic displays: birth, death, age, sex, race, class, employment, income, education, marital status, etc. These attributes are also clues to index entry concepts as heads or modifications. Third, neither cases nor interviews are of themselves a source of clues to index material. The clues to index entry material are in the concept that the cases and interviews illustrate. Fourth, the vocabulary of the social science disciplines beyond the social studies level contains numerous complex phrases that must be treated as a unit and not inverted. A few simple examples will illustrate the point: *anthropology*, accident of variation, amity-enmity complex; Dissolution of Central Position, predatory transition; *psychology*, achievement motivation, ambiguity in perception, problem-centered thinking, frame of reference, selective learning; *economics*, acceleration principle, balance of payments, factors of production, factor pricing.

The choice of an index pattern for a work in the social sciences depends on the orientation—toward science or toward social analysis (theory) and criticism. For example, a major text on economics, with extensive treatment of microeconomics and needed sub-modifications, is best suited to the line-by-line pattern. A critique of the Austrian school of economics, on the other hand, could be fitted into a paragraphed format. Political science also seems to favor the paragraphed format. Sociology and psychology, being fields with terms and concepts heavy with meaning, do well in the line-by-line pattern.

A special situation in social science indexing is the legal text. Such a work concerned with cases and statutes may require a separate table of cases, with special rules for style and format.

Legal indexing is full of pitfalls: Latin and French phrases are common; a term used in different contexts may have different meanings, as may a term in the singular and the plural form. The indexer must follow the text religiously and be wary of terms that seem to be similar (and might be brought together under a single head), but actually have distinctly different meanings. Obviously, the indexer must be especially qualified for this work.

In religion, usage and style (problems of capitals or lower case) differ among different faiths and denominations. There is no difficulty with works directed to a single faith or religion; inconsistencies are the only challenge. However, in comparative religion, where several faiths or denominations are compared, alternative terms should be entered in the index with appropriate cross-references.

A characteristic of social science text is redundancy. Discussions of a single concept from multiple theoretical viewpoints results in terms being repeated in contexts where their importance is only illustrative. Movement of the exposition in such a text is not forward but circular. The problem, as it concerns the indexer, is which mention in the text of a concept (term) is relevant and which insignificant. To avoid the accumulation of page numbers for which there are no meaningful modifications, the indexer must immediately set criteria of importance: which references to a concept (term) are to be included and which omitted. Also, if modifications are consistently provided for the included concepts as entries are written up, the shocking discovery of terms followed by strings of page numbers will be avoided when the index is finally assembled.

TEXTBOOKS AND REFERENCE WORKS

In the printing and publishing business the sector with the largest capitalization, highest gross income, largest output, largest market, and most workers is the textbook and reference work sector. For textbooks the market for books begins in preschool and extends through to adult education and to graduate divisions of the university. The subjects covered defy precise definition; it might be said that no subject has not been in some textbook or reference work. However, one aspect of the material can be categorized, and that is the depth and manner of presentation, the classifying criteria being the age and the educational attainment of the prospective user.

One characteristic that distinguishes all books in this large category is the importance of the fact. One refers to a reference work for a specific piece of information: for a fact classified as general knowledge: facts, right facts, all the facts determined by "experts" to be appropriate to the user's level of understanding. Factual inaccuracy brings criticism from every quarter. Another characteristic is the "voice of authority," the reputation of the authors of textbooks and of contributors and consultants to reference works. The upshot is that teachers are naturals for jobs in textbook publishing, and editors academically equipped in a specific subject for work on encyclopedic references.

In both textbooks and reference works the facts are arranged in a familiar pattern. In textbooks the facts are presented in "lessons" progressing in difficulty, with questions and answers, and accompanied by figures, charts, diagrams, "boxes," and illustrations. Encyclopedic reference works are arranged alphabetically; reference works limited to a single subject may be arranged topically as well as alphabetically. For elementary- and high-school (el-hi) textbooks, ancillary publications are part of the package: workbooks, study guides, teachers' manuals, prospectus for salespeople, and audiovisual aids.

For textbooks, the criteria for indexes are clear: the age of the user and the aims of the authors and editors are the most important guides. In textbooks for the elementary school, the concepts are simple, and the vocabulary is limited. For the indexer the organization of the text provides the needed clues. Headings are numerous and contain the concepts (terms) to be stressed. Exercises, questions, and summaries reinforce indexing decisions. A vocabulary list (definitions) is a further enhancer. Textbooks for high schools follow the same general organization, with tables and graphs, questions, summaries, and sometimes projects.

Again, college textbooks vary little, with more graphic material, conclusions, summaries, questions for discussion, and sometimes appendices to chapters.

However, el-hi textbooks in one respect are fundamentally different. Members of college and university faculties can choose and often write their own textbooks. In elementary and secondary education, choosing the textbooks is not a teacher's prerogative. A special arm of the textbook publishing business is a highly organized and trained sales force. (The same is true of encyclopedia publishing.) El-hi textbooks are "adopted." States, and in some instances municipalities, through government-appointed adoption committees, decide which books will be bought and used in the public schools throughout the state or municipality. All texts must meet the standards of state-approved curricula. A textbook must also meet manufacturing standards and specifications established by NASTA—National Association of State Textbook Administrators; these specifications cover all aspects of production, particularly binding materials. (Parochial schools use different methods to purchase textbooks, all of which must meet curriculum standards set by the church authority.)

The purchaser of el-hi textbooks is a professional buyer, with a committee of educators and bureaucrats to convince. The sales material for the textbook salesperson's "pitch" is a prospectus, heavy with the use of color and illustration to make the book he or she is pushing look as good as possible. In all textbook markets there is a complex web of academic purchasers, administrators, and influential teachers that the salesperson has to reach and persuade.

An important factor in the successful adoption of a textbook is whether it is well received by professional organizations and reviewers. It should be apparent by this time that anything that mars a textbook's image can be fatal to a publisher trying to win against competitors with adoption committees. And a poor index can be just such a blemish. For this reason an indexer of an el-hi textbook must be prepared to work within limits imposed on content and format.

As noted earlier, el-hi textbooks are well organized with numerous center heads and side heads, illustrations, and graphic material, which provide the indexer with sound clues to concepts. The line-by-line format is easily followed and is particularly adapted to the large number of single-word terms with few modifications. The one "catch" is that of available space. For elementary textbooks the index is limited to one to three percent of the text; for high school textbooks, the range is five to eight percent. Salespeople sell a textbook of a specific size, which means number of pages of particular format. However, editors and indexers of el-hi textbooks adjust to these restrictions.

All encyclopedias require indexes, and in view of the magnitude of the encyclopedia publishing business, the importance of that fact to indexers should be obvious. Multivolume encyclopedias, like textbooks, are sold by sales organizations which have the same aim as textbook salespeople: convincing institutional buyers (libraries, schools, etc.) but also individuals (parents) of the superiority of the product. A prospectus is also part of the sales package. And as is true of textbooks, an index can affect approval by individual buyers and influential reviewers. These potential difficulties can usually be preempted by major encyclopedia publishers: A standing encyclopedia has been refined in revisions over many editions, with established criteria for concept selection and a fixed format and style. As events provide new facts to be added to the text, the index as well as the text is changed in ongoing revisions.

A general encyclopedia requires the same decisions as any text, with one exception—the alphabetical arrangement of entries, and the mandatory succinctness of the entry heads: persons, places, things, events—already in place when the page proof is ready for indexing. Thus encyclopedia entry heads become *index* entry heads. The object of text analysis in encyclopedia indexing is to isolate *additional* concepts for entry heads as well as to flush out the substance of the standing index entries.

Whether the format is line-by-line or paragraphed is decided by the publisher; generally, the line-by-line pattern is preferred because it produces more pages of index. For a multivolume encyclopedia a special style is needed for the page-number keys. The *volume number* of an index must be combined with the page number. The volume number is often in bold face with the page number(s) in Roman (**10**: 946–950). Other codes and styles are set up for illustrations and plates.

The production of an index for a new multivolume encyclopedia is a major undertaking. A method is proposed in chapter 2, ''Technique.''

SUMMARY

Because disciplines are not just different in subject matter but in how the practitioners regard their subjects and the means that are used for study and reporting, an indexer has something to be gained from knowing these differences and individual approaches. This chapter places the disciplines into three different groups: science, humanities, and social science. A third group, textbook and reference work publishing, is also included because of the special nature of the indexing methodology.

The salient points in indexing methodology of books on science and technology have to do with the effect of scientific research methods on the assembling of research data and the reporting of research results. In the reporting, tables, graphs and illustrations contain all relevant data. The manuscript explains these data and the results and offers an explanation for the findings.

This standard organization of a research report carries over into the organization of collateral or derived scientific publications, which use the accumulated research results on a subject as the basis, for example, of a monograph or a textbook. For the indexer this generally used model for the scientific literature has a structure useful in identifying concepts: graphic material, center heads, side heads, illustrations, and traditional parts: for example, abstract, introduction, description of research methods, data analysis, and summary or conclusions.

In terms of an indexing methodology for the disciplines making up the humanities, there is no unifying viewpoint to make possible a definitive statement as to general goals or content organization. Accordingly, the indexer must look for distinguishing features of the individual disciplines. However, the one commonality is the occurrence of proper nouns—people, places, things, events, works. These nouns are valid concepts for entries by themselves and also in combination, as with modifications.

The terminology of the humanities, particularly criticism, where the writer may deal with theory and "schools," is often multiterm and obscure. Such works are often not thought to need an index, or the author prepares it himself.

Unlike the scientific disciplines, where tests and measurements are carried out with physical (nonhuman) instruments, in the social sciences, tests and measurements are performed by the human research observer. As a consequence of this difference, the social science disciplines have no unified underpinning of accepted "truths." The disciplines are characterized by conflicting theories and "schools." For the indexer this means that each discipline must be approached in terms of its individual peculiarities. Accordingly, while in some instances the organization of the text is somewhat similar to works in the physical sciences—with graphic displays and structured format with heads—in other instances, particularly those advancing the cause of a theory or "school," the text is without an orienting structure for the indexer.

In the textbook and reference work publishing business, the market and marketing drive the engine. The textbook arm of this business operates under a set of "game" rules that control distribution. Textbooks for public schools are not "bought" but "adopted." States and some municipalities buy books through the instrument of an adoption committee with the assistance of "professional" buyers, who examine competing textbooks to determine whether they conform to the curriculum approved by the state or municipality.

In this highly competitive atmosphere, with many textbook publishers participating, the textbook salesperson plays a key role. And to support these efforts, the textbook publisher not only pays close attention to the standards set by the adoption complex but also to a textbook format (appearance) that will be effective against competing textbook publishers—such pluses as appealing illustration and color, as well as graphic material.

The standard format, whether for el-hi or higher education texts, is organized around heads, graphic material, introduction, summary, and ancillary sections such as exercises. All these features provide the indexer with clues for entry concepts. A limiting factor for el-hi textbooks is the predetermined size, with a specified number of pages allotted to the index.

Encyclopedias likewise have a definite structure, which provides unequivocal clues for entry concepts: the entries themselves, arranged alphabetically, become index entry heads; substance is added to this basic framework from entries on related subjects throughout the encyclopedia. Unlike the textbook, the encyclopedia has no limits to index length, comprising as it does a separate volume. The multivolume aspect of an encyclopedia requires a special style for page number keys, which must also include a volume number.

Recommendations in this chapter for format and style are those that have been found to be user friendly. For each discipline the kinds of problems likely to be encountered are spelled out.

CHAPTER 9

FREELANCE INDEXING

Freelance indexers are an important feature of the publishing scene. While in-house indexing is appropriate for series and multivolume works, and while some authors (with the publisher's approval) opt to prepare their own indexes, most publishers turn to freelance indexers for quality indexes delivered on time.

For the indexer-publisher (or indexer-author) relationship to be satisfactory, both must benefit. The publisher must get a good index on time at a fair price. And the indexer must so manage the enterprise as to have a work flow at fees that promise a profit. This chapter covers the business practices that foster a satisfactory indexer-client relationship.

The would-be freelance indexer faces several obstacles: how to get training—to learn how to do it—and then how to get enough experience to make a freelance operation feasible. Unlike other careers in book publishing, for example, editing, proofreading, layout, production—all of which are offered in an academic setting or in workshops as well as in publishing firms as hands-on training—opportunities for learning how to index are limited. There are two reasons. To take the second point first: for hands-on training in a publishing firm, the required steady flow of work just does not exist for indexing. As has been pointed out in chapter 1, who indexes any specific book is likely to be determined by the author, who may decide to do it him- or herself. Also, the scheduling of books to provide a steady flow of work for an in-house indexer is an impossibility in the real world of publishing. In fact, back-of-book indexing and the independent contractor—freelance indexer—are made for each other.

The one place where professional training may be obtained is in schools of library science, where indexing is considered an essential skill for a librarian. One non-institutional course is offered by the USDA, the only one currently available in the United States. Otherwise opportunities for training are limited to workshops provided from time to time by professional organizations, such as the American Society of Indexers.

There is also the question whether indexing can be taught, or whether like so many technical skills, it must be learned by doing. Although there are rules for alphabetization, format organization, and styling and an approach to index methodology and technique that will illuminate the step-by-step operations that make up the skill (chapters 1 and 2), these operations are best learned by doing, preferably while receiving on-the-job training. This kind of training is available in firms that have indexes undergoing continuous revision, such as publishers of major encyclopedias, yearbooks, and looseleaf publications, or in an indexing service. Obviously, the indexers most likely to succeed as freelancers are those who have had some experience in a publishing house or an indexing service.

Reinforcing the chances of success are specialization (such as medical, legal, or technical indexing) and an academic degree to back up the specialization claims. Two basic questions about freelancing are: why take the plunge and when should the move be made? Abandoning a full-time job for self-employment has risks that must be compensated for by personal or financial gain. Since no freelance indexer got rich from indexing, the initial motivation is usually personal as well as financial. Aging and looming retirement, with the prospect of having to live on Social Security or a pension, make self-employment as an indexer an attractive means of finding supplemental income.

A more serious matter is when to make the change without financial shock. It is entirely feasible for an experienced indexer to start a freelance business while still employed. Making the most of contacts within the publishing business over several years will begin to build a viable business. A good source of potential clients is the *Literary Market Place,* which publishes names, addresses, and phone numbers, as well as each publisher's annual output and areas of specialization. An exploratory letter should list the indexer's qualifications and experience and should also include a complete résumé.

There are some side issues that should not be ignored. Where the freelancer lives can make the difference between financial success and failure. Fees and promptness of payment vary among publishers. Business overhead expenses (housing, utilities, insurance, supplies, etc.) are greater in metropolitan areas in the north-east, for example, than in the mid-south.

A viable freelance business depends in no small part on choosing and establishing good relations with reliable publisher clients. The ideal publisher client is one who recognizes the importance of an index to the success of a publication and appreciates the work of a competent indexer, has reasonable deadlines, delivers proof on schedule, has a fair pay scale, and pays promptly. Such clients do exist; in fact, they are in the majority. An important link in the indexer-publisher relationship is the in-house staff member in charge of indexing, usually the managing editor or an editor in charge of all aspects of indexing. Making friends with these staffers is essential.

The indexer-author relationship is another matter. Authors for whom the publisher makes an arrangement with an indexer (1) may have definite ideas about what should be in the index, (2) may have started the index themselves and now want someone else to finish it, or (3) complain that the finished index does not do justice to their book. Since the author is charged for the index through royalties, the publisher may feel obliged to cater to the author's wishes. The indexer naturally favors a publisher who successfully mediates such a dispute. When an author makes an arrangement with an indexer directly, the indexer should be particularly careful about the details of the negotiation.

Negotiations with both publisher and author should cover: subject and length of the text to be indexed, proof delivery schedule, and deadline for delivery of the manuscript. Fees are often a matter for negotiation. The author who contracts with an indexer is acting as a go-between in the arrangement, and some of the details may be fuzzy. Usually in such instances the whole set of page proof is sent to the indexer. (For computer-assisted indexing the negotiations also involve procedures for delivery of camera-ready copy or a disk of typescript.) Some indexers favor a written contract with the publisher to fix conditions of payment.

The test of indexer-publisher relations comes when things go wrong. Then a sense of humor and self-control are essential. Helping a managing editor get off the hook when page proofs are not only delayed but flawed with makeup error—and the scheduled delivery to production is just days away—can pay dividends, even though it may mean working overtime at top speed.

Once in a while the indexer will come across a nitpicking in-house index editor, sold on the idea that indexes are syntactical constructs, that every modification should have a relating preposition or conjunction. Nothing is to be gained by refuting the false assumption.

Temperament for self-employment should not be overlooked in the exuberance of becoming one's own boss. An indexer opting out of the regime of company-based employment may discover an inability to function outside a controlled environment. Accordingly, one should test oneself by taking on indexing jobs while still employed and by this means become conditioned to scheduling regular hours of work.

From the outset, the indexer should keep a record of each client's name, address, and phone number and the *person to contact*. The turnover in publishing is such that today's supervisor of indexers may not be there tomorrow.

The file should include copies of clients' style guides and sample indexes and any correspondence detailing requirements for billing and for mailing manuscript.

Not all clients are desirable. An indexer does well to consider the advisability of keeping clients who fail to honor proof delivery schedules, make changes in text proof requiring revisions in the index without adjusting payment or deadlines, and remit reluctantly. When a remittance is delayed for more than thirty days, the indexer should ask whether the client is really worth it.

Once the indexer is established, the advisability of seeking new clients must always be weighed against the needs and expectations of the old ones. A good part of the satisfaction and financial success in freelance indexing comes from the skillful juggling of commitments to deserving clients within a limited time frame.

At the same time it is unwise to depend too much on one or two clients, even though the financial returns are good and the relationship satisfactory. Publishers go out of business and firms merge; staffs change; new managers and editors may have their own cadre of indexers from another job. It is always useful to have the names of additional prospective clients in reserve.

Being specific about the basis for calculating indexing charges is essential. Rates as well as the basis for calculating charges vary among publishers, and records must be kept to cover these variations. Hourly rates often depend on the location of the publishing house. The hours per work week are regulated by labor laws, and arrangements must be made with the publisher for overtime. The record should show the hours worked daily, charges being calculated from the total. A per entry rate is usually based on the number of entry heads and modifications, seldom on the number of page references. The entries are totaled and the fee is calculated when the manuscript is finished. The text page rate (for example, two or three dollars per page) is based on the *numbered* text pages. If material in the appendices is to be indexed, those pages are included, but not pages of glossary, notes, or bibliography. The number of pages is recorded, and the fee is calculated when the final proof is received. A manuscript page rate is based on an 8-1/2″ by 11″ sheet with the index being typed to space, that is, so many characters per line and lines per page. The fee is calculated and recorded when the index is finished. A flat rate may be requested from an indexer when the publisher is going to charge the indexing to the author or against the author's royalties, and the author wants to know "how much." An experienced indexer can often quote a fair price just by knowing the length of the text, the size of the text page (one, two, or three columns), and the subject matter. (Knowing the number of probable entries per column or page for the subject makes the calculation fairly simple.) However, such a fee commitment should always be accompanied by a warning that atypical indexing situations may warrant additional charges.

How the indexer handles the materials for indexing received from the publisher may make the difference between a stressful and a stress-free indexing business. The first step is to check the proof delivered for (1) continuity with prior deliveries, (2) missing pages, (3) improperly numbered pages, (4) missing illustrations, and (5) improperly numbered illustrations. Changes forwarded by the publisher should be incorporated in the proof immediately, not put aside until the passage is to be indexed.

The indexer's greatest asset is time well managed, and the dovetailing of one indexing assignment with another is the key to staying in business. On the one hand, the indexer must be prepared to compensate for late delivery of proof or the substitution of galley for promised page proof. On the other hand, the indexer should look on an early delivery of proof as a bonus, as an opportunity to profit from efficient time management. By not putting off processing the proof because the deadline has not been advanced, the indexer can often squeeze in that "extra" job.

All proof and preliminary index entry copy should be kept until the job has been delivered and acknowledged and payment received. Then all index entry copy (cards, slips, manuscript) should be destroyed. There is a real danger that cards or slips from one index may get mixed up with those for another if files are not thoroughly cleaned out.

A factor over which the indexer has no control is error in the delivered proof, mainly misspellings, inconsistency in significant terminology, and gross grammatical blunders. At one time a listing of such error discovered during indexing was forwarded to the publisher with the index manuscript. Today, however, production technology allows "imperfect" proof to be delivered to the indexer, sometimes photocopy of pasteups. Since such proof will be undergoing in-house proofreading at the same time as the index is being written, the publisher will not appreciate useless notes about typographical error. However, inconsistency and errors that affect the content of the index should be noted, either on the index manuscript or in a covering memorandum.

A posted schedule of indexing commitments ensures against failures in a number of areas. Such a schedule should carry the client's name, title of the work being indexed, date due, date mailed, charges billed, and date remittance is received. At a glance the indexer can tell (1) whether another assignment can be worked into the schedule, (2) how well the work is progressing toward the deadline, and (3) when a remittance should be expected.

Client	Title	Due	Mailed	Charges	Remittance

Time management may make the difference between a profitable business venture and a disaster. Fundamentally, time is what everyone (not just the freelance indexer) has to sell. Even with just a few clients—fewer than fill the time the indexer wishes to devote to indexing—time mismanagement cuts into time available for other necessary or leisure activity. With a full roster of clients, time mismanagement will invariably result in mediocre work, destructive stress, and failure to meet deadlines.

To keep track of progress toward a deadline, time needed for each step in index preparation is projected—for preliminary survey, marking copy (particularly for a typist), entry construction, entry checking, alphabetization, editing and styling, manuscript preparation, and final checking. For different subjects, these time slots may differ. Such a projection is most important when several indexes are being worked on at the same time or when contemplating additional work. With experience, the indexer need only see page proof and make a preliminary survey to delegate time for each step and project index length and cost.

Several other features of time management need to be mentioned: what to do when a mental block occurs and time is fleeing? Put the passage aside; it is not going anywhere. And turn to another task, or take a break. Walk about for five minutes, make a drink, start a meal, or do some laundry, and then go back to the passage that caused the block. Look at what precedes it and what follows: almost invariably the solution will be revealed. When such a block occurs at the end of the day, as it often does, there is no harm in sleeping on it and attacking the passage the first thing in the morning. Pacing the work on an index without wasting time is an important aspect of time management.

One of the advantages of freelancing is having a choice of working hours. A night person who finds daytime office hours deadly may work all night. A day person, particularly one who is up with the birds, may get in a full day's work by noon and have the rest of the day for other activity.

How money is managed is as important as how much is made. Net income is not the same as gross income; it is what is left after expenses and determines whether a business is viable. A freelancer should learn early that what seems to be a minor expenditure can, when multiplied, add up to a major liability, that expensive equipment appropriate for a well-equipped office is not needed to do a quality indexing job.

For indexing on cards or strips and the preparation of a typed manuscript, the following expenditures for equipment, supplies, and services should be expected: office space, utilities, equipment including repairs, materials (paper, cards, file boxes, typewriter ribbons, envelopes), postage, telephone, travel, typist's assistance, and accountant's fee.

For the preparation of electronic manuscript, different and

more expensive equipment and additional supplies are required. Furthermore, the calculation of whether or not the operation is profitable is more complex. The business advantages of computer-assisted indexing are two: (1) satisfying the requirement of the publisher for electronic manuscript and (2) reducing time spent on keyboarding, filing, and copy preparation. If the time saved can be filled with additional business and the fees charged can be large enough to compensate for the more expensive operation, the business will be profitable. If neither the work load nor the fees meet these conditions, the undertaking may be disappointing.

Records of income and expenditures are needed for two reasons: for computing taxes and determining the profitability of the business. Indexing has been described as a ''cottage'' industry; the indexer works at home. Income tax laws permit a specifically defined (measured) area of home to be designated ''office.'' This space as a percentage of the whole is the basis for computing deductions for rent and utilities. Totals for payment of rent and utilities may be computed from checks and receipts at the end of the tax year. However, a running record should be kept of all other expenditures as well as income. A notebook serves very well as a ledger.

For expenditures each entry should include the date, description of the item, and amount. For income the entry should include date, client's name, and amount of remittance. A properly kept ledger shows where the money is coming from and going, the difference being an indication of the health of the freelancing business.

SUMMARY

Freelance indexing is a viable means of self-employment *if* the indexer (1) is well-trained and experienced and has specialized, (2) uses indexing to supplement a full-time job, (3) upon retirement lives in a locale where income from indexing is adequate if added to a pension or Social Security, (4) has the temperament and self-discipline to produce according to a self-imposed schedule, and (5) manages time and money frugally. With the possible exception of some lowering of living standards, the advantages far outweigh the disadvantages. Relatively speaking, one's time is one's own. Working time and leisure time can be mixed in a number of ways, working in the early morning hours or late at night. Vacation time is flexible, not being subject to company rules and schedules. The risk of becoming "unemployed" or "underemployed" is hardly greater than with a company-based job in periods of retrenchment.

Finally, a few caveats. It doesn't pay to be greedy. Getting too big, taking on more assignments than can be comfortably and satisfactorily completed, will lead to commitment failures and loss of clients. No commitment should be made that cannot be kept. Despite pressure from a client, the indexer should not hesitate to say "no."

CHAPTER 10

COMPUTER-ASSISTED INDEXING

The computer revolution has dramatically changed many processes of communication, including the fundamentals of the printing and publishing industry, with repercussions not only in the factors of production (labor and capital) but also in the basic elements of publication production, from copy keyboarding through copy editing, and copy formating, to printing and binding. The computer has become ubiquitous.

Back-of-book indexing has not escaped, mainly because of the invention of the personal computer (PC). Beginning in 1972 with an exploratory application of the computer to the automation of index formatting display (printing), automation technology for indexing has undergone continuous development, leading to specialized computer software for back-of-book indexing.

Automation has also affected standards that indirectly affect indexing. For example, the American Library Association's filing rules have been revised to eliminate some traditional usages in alphabetizing and ordering that could not be automated.

While at this stage in software development, collating, deletions, and insertions, styling and formatting are all automated, intellectual input is still needed for higher levels of ordering and editing. Also, the computer will not correct mistakes other than in the general run of spelling error; software is not capable of correcting error in scientific and technical terms and in variant spellings, homophones (yoke, yolk), and proper names. Nor will it correct wrong page numbers and wrong coding directives.

For the freelance indexer, the attractions of computer-assisted indexing are probably twofold: (1) elimination of the tedious detail of typing cards or strips, of alphabetizing and ordering, and of typing up final manuscript; and (2) the resultant saving of time, which, used to solicit additional clients, translates into more money. Realistically, the calculation should also include the cost and maintenance of computer hardware, software, and supplies, and the possibility that new clients may not be all that easy to get. The freelancer speculating about converting to computer-assisted indexing should also consider the personality factor of compatibility with the machine after forming habits with other indexing techniques. (See also chapter 9, "Freelance Indexing.")

The rest of this chapter describes the step-by-step development of computer-assisted indexing and its current status.

The application of computer technology to indexing has undergone three phases. The first was the use of automation only to format and display (compose and print) a humanly prepared index written in a word-processor file. In the second phase the indexing was computer-prepared or computer-assisted. The input consisted of (1) automatically selected key terms from a title (or section of text—KWIC methodology) or (2) humanly assigned key terms. Such input was formatted and displayed as the final index. In the third phase software was developed to assist in the detail of preparing a book index from publisher's proof (DIPS—dedicated indexing programs). Any list of what a computer program can do is impressive:

1. Ordering—e.g., alphabetizing
2. Sorting and collating
3. Selecting—e.g., synonym search
4. Editing—checking, correcting, suppressing
5. Storing and retrieving
6. Interpreting and translating
7. Coding for formatting and typesetting

Basic to any of these applications is software compatible with the desired index content and format and with computer hardware.

But far and above all other considerations is that computer assistance be faster and less costly than the intellectual and clerical processing of the same material.

In the first application it was recognized that for one class of indexes—the annual indexes for scientific and technical periodicals—computer software could be developed to handle the tedious task of keyword selection for entry heads of titles (KWIC), followed by alphabetization and ordering. However, such computer-generated indexes had limitations, and in subsequent refinements the input was humanly selected, the computer being used as an indexing aid. Application of optical character recognition (OCR) technology for humanly selected input, and computer-driven formatting and composition (photocomposition), led to improved efficiency.

Perhaps the most extensive applications of computerized word indexing are in the KWIC (*key word in context*) and KWOC (*key word out of context*) methodologies. H. P. Luhn reported in 1959 on the KWIC indexing method for extracting key terms from publication titles for annual indexes for the technical (scientific) literature. The technology also included the automation of the clerical tasks of ordering (alphabetization). The keyword designator (cursor) is situated in the middle of the electronic manuscript page of titles. Each keyword is rotated into an entry position. (A stopword list—a list of common or insignificant words stored in machine-readable form—forbids the filing of words that are trivial.) Each publication title appears as many times as there are keywords in the title. One line of context (limited by the character count of the display line) is allowed for each index entry. With title recirculation (wrap around) in the rotation process, the end of the title may precede the beginning. The KWIC format (printout) (also known as string indexing) is achieved by alphabetically aligning the keywords with associated text.

biosynthesis of *apolipoprotein B* in rooster kidney intestine and liver
tine and liver *biosynthesis* of apolipoprotein B in rooster kidney intes
rooster kidney *intestine* and liver biosynthesis of apolipoprotein B in
B in rooster *kidney* intestine and liver biosynthesis of apoplipoprotein
intestine and *liver* biosynthesis of apolipoprotein B in rooster kidney
poprotein B in *rooster* kidney intestine and liver biosynthesis of apoli

Although originally computer generated, KWIC indexing was subsequently refined and modified to be computer-assisted with intellectual (human) input. Intermediate steps were double KWIC and KWOC (*key word out of context*).

The double KWIC technology calls for the generation of subordinate entries (modifications) for each main key term in the title (or portion of a text). After the main (key) term is extracted, the remaining (qualifying) significant terms are rotated and displayed under the main term. Index entries are then formatted alphabetically by main (key) terms and within the sequence of modifying terms. This ordering produces a printout in the conventional index format.

With KWOC (*key word out of context*) technology, the key term, selected by designator (cursor) from the title (or text of a document), is displayed on the left-hand margin of the format, followed by the full title or textual content in unaltered sequence (in contrast with the KWIC arrangement). Meaningless words are suppressed, as with KWIC. A keyword that appears in more than one title is displayed only once, with full titles (including bibliographical details) being listed alphabetically under the key term by the first word in the full title.

With refinements the KWIC (KWOC) technology has been converted from computer-generated to computer-assisted indexing to produce AKWIC (*author and key word in context*), WADEX (*word author index*), and AKWAS (*author and key words in alphabetical sequence*). Examples of such applications are to indexes for *Applied Mechanical Reviews, Biological Abstracts, Bibliography of Agriculture,* and the NASA Bibliographic series.

Similar technology has been used in computer-assisted indexing and formatting of catalogues, bibliographies, directories, and so on.

When key terms and modifications are intellectually selected, computer function is limited to routine and clerical tasks and formatting and printing the final index. These clerical and routine operations in manipulating intellectually selected input are: ordering, checking for consistency and completeness, adding cross-references, and checking input vocabulary against a thesaurus (word list) in machine-readable form. Computer editing of electronic manuscript (aided by a machine-readable thesaurus) reveals inconsistent spelling and singular and plural forms and can substitute preferred terms for synonyms (with generation of indicated cross-references).

Along with the positive aspects of the foregoing computer-generated and computer-aided indexing processes are advantages for specific applications: (1) For cumulative indexes, the computer file makes possible efficient maintenance, search (interrogation), and updating without reprocessing previous data. (2) In addition to subject indexes, such ancillary indexes as author, title, and word indexes and bibliographies are feasible computer applications. (3) Assistance is provided the indexer in key term selection, error identification, and amendment and updating of the computer file.

The described applications of computer-assisted indexing are well established for periodical annual and cumulative indexes, directories, bibliographies, and so on. Other feasible applications are to multivolume works and reference works with a relatively fixed vocabulary and that are subject to revision (updating and error correction), definite benefit-deriving from computer storage. All these applications of computer-assisted indexing are for large indexing projects characterized by the clerical (routine) processing of massive amounts of material.

For word-processor (WPBI) book indexing, two kinds of software programs are available. In one the index is prepared on a word processor, as it would be applicable to desk-top publishing. With the cursor (designator) of the word processor, both single and multiple-word key terms are selected for the file. The computer then formats the index with the proper page numbers attached to the terms selected. An example is the XyWrite program that performs the function of ordering, alphabetizing, cross-referencing, and formatting. In another application of this kind of program, a preselected list of key terms is entered with the order to search the data file and record the occurrence and page numbers for the terms, followed by manipulation (alphabetizing and so on) into an index format. Such indexes are edited from the printout and corrected before typesetting. The principal use for this type of program is for word indexing, especially indexes of places, titles, person's names, and terms.

Since the pages in the electronic file do not correspond to the pages of the typeset proof, the software should have the capability of repaginating the files to correspond to the typeset pages. This requires that once the page proofs are available, the pages in the index file be broken down into numbered increments to correspond to the pages of the typeset proof—a time-consuming task.

With the second kind of software program for book indexing (dedicated indexing programs—DIPS), the index is prepared on the word processor with the publisher's page proofs, as it would be on cards or strips, the computer taking care of ordering, alphabetizing, formatting, and printing. The methodology is the same as for an index prepared on cards or strips.

However, in the areas of alphabetization and order, indexing technique has been changed by the introduction of computer technology. To meet the requirements of simplification and standardization, the American Library Association published new filing rules in 1980.

The first of such software programs appeared in 1982. Programs currently available are compatible with the IBM PC computer or Macintosh systems. These programs vary considerable in price and capability for sorting, editing, displaying entries, and formatting. In general, the programs provide assistance in alphabetizing, either word by word or letter by letter; formatting in line-by-line or run-in style; suppression of repeated heads and subheads; merging of page references; and provision of at least two subheads (but may provide many more). The software for book indexing is undergoing continuous improvement. A detailed analysis of available software is published by the American Society of Indexers and is kept current with updating.

The final preparation and submission of electronic manuscript to the publisher may involve coding, whether or not the index is computer-assisted or only prepared on the word processor for electronic typesetting. Two codes for marking up electronic index manuscript are in use at the present time: The University of Chicago Press developed its own code for generic markup of electronic manuscript, described in the *Chicago Guide to Preparing Electronic Manuscripts*. The other style was developed by the Association of American Publishers.

These codes are used to mark up the electronic manuscript for heads, typeface (e.g., italics), format, special characters (foreign languages, mathematical symbols), and so on. Uncoded manuscript requires the compositor to insert the required codes one at a time; with coded electronic manuscript the compositor is able in one operation to replace the generic codes with those required for electronic typesetting. The indexer who undertakes to code the electronic manuscript for typesetting should find out ahead of time which code the publisher prefers. (Some details of formatting are taken care of by the typesetting computer.) When the printout and computer files are sent to the publisher, they should be accompanied by complete information about the hardware and software used in preparing the index. The indexer should add five to ten percent to the indexing charges for coding electronic manuscript.

If electronic manuscript is to be considered for revision, the publisher must be sure the version to be used (author's or typesetter's) contains all the corrections. Extensive revisions using the author's copy may involve expensive technical conversion.

An instructive example of a computer-assisted methodology in index preparation for a multivolume scholarly edition is that for a comprehensive edition of *The Papers of Henry Laurens* at the University of South Carolina. The project, using CINDEX, had the objective of a comprehensive index to the publication of about 12,000 documents by Laurens in fifteen volumes. Projected index items for the cumulative index were in the neighborhood of 45,000 cards for merging and editing. About half the indexing terms appeared in the text; the rest were supplied by the editors. Terms in the text were underlined; created terms were noted in the margins of the page proof. The selected terms were then keyboarded directly from marked page proof onto a CRT. The data entry form provided for the page number to be keyed in once, followed by the string of relevant index items. Precedence codes were used for page numbers, main entries, and modifications. Cross-references and volume references were other index features. Computer storage provided for file updating to ensure consistency. Codes were also provided for computerized typesetting. With the creation of a structured data file, the sorted and collated raw data could be edited, followed by resorting and a printout in final form. The data file was stored for use in creating a cumulative index.

SUMMARY

Unquestionably, the computer is here to stay as a permanent fixture in the publishing industry. What the future holds is unpredictable. With the explosion of innovations in telecommunication technology, current computer hardware and software may be expected to undergo innumerable modifications with their replacement in time.

Computer-assisted indexing as part of the computer revolution has proved its value in specific areas, including back-of-book indexing, as indicated by the current capabilities of the technology.

1. Alphabetization and ordering: word by word and letter by letter, with nonsorting capability for letters and words.
2. Formatting: line by line or paragraphed, with settings for column width and indentations.
3. Type styling capability for all standard as well as special characters.
4. Suppression of headings and subheadings.
5. Page number (locator) ordering.
6. Coding for electronic manuscript.

On the other hand, the computer has not replaced the intellectual process of "thinking" indexing, nor is it likely to in the future. Like the typewriter and other equipment associated with indexing techniques, the computer is a *tool,* the successful use of that tool depending not on the capabilities of the computer but on those of the indexer.

AFTERWORD

Whatever the focus of individual writers on indexes and indexing, the indexer remains undefined and, according to some, undervalued. However, if one considers the indexer's fringe position and indefinite status in the publishing scene and the modest return for considerable skill, questions about identity and value become understandable. These questions might be posited as: What does the indexer do (the process)? Why is it done (the purpose)? And what is the significance (the meaning)?

But first, how to account for the marginal position and the modest financial return. Part of the reason lies in the nature of the work, some in the organization and economics of the publishing business, and some in the tenuous relationship between indexer and publishing house staff, the author, and the index user—the "searcher." And finally in the nature of the indexer: his/her view of a congenial life-style, identification with the work, and the satisfaction found in it in relation to its demands and its rewards.

It is unfortunate that an index is so easily identified by its form: a list of words alphabetically arranged, followed by number keys. Common experience with the index form in the phone book and other familiar reference sources supports the idea that an index is really a very simple construct. And it is but a step from such ordinary experiences to conclude that something so simple must be simple to make and that anybody can do it.

But an index is *not* a "list of words" but an organization of concepts: word symbols for the substance of the author's thesis as traced in the prose of the text. The grammatical form of these concepts is the *substantive*—a noun or noun phrase. What the indexer does—the process—combines research with planning, then analysis, then synthesis, and finally formatting (design)—all moving toward a known end: the conversion of concepts is one

145

form in the text into concepts in another form (entries) in the index. This is hardly the common perception of an onlooker. It is only when we abandon the notion of an index as being made up of "words" and move to the acceptance of concepts (substantives) as the real material of index entries, that the true nature of an index and indexing becomes clear.

With the abandonment of the index as a "word list" the corollary notion that "anyone can do it" must also be abandoned. These notions must be replaced with the acceptance of indexing as a multifaceted process and of back-of-book indexing as a skill requiring an appropriate background of education, training, and experience.

Nearly all serious books calling for back-of-book indexes are "discipline derived." This implies familiarity with a discipline's special terminology: Latin taxonomy for the biological sciences; nomenclature for elements and compounds, including symbols and abbreviations, for the physical sciences; coinages for theoretical constructs in the humanities and social sciences.

On the surface the technical details of the indexing process after entry construction are simple: filing for purposes of alphabetization and ordering, arranging for formatting, marking up for style. In fact these operations often require choices among alternatives for the precise differentiation of homographs and for the organization of atypical material. To provide guidance, rules and standards have been proposed by interested organizations.

In 1980, after the advent of computer technology, the American Library Association promulgated new *Filing Rules* to provide a standard for bibliographic records; the standard has been accepted as a guide for attaining consistency in back-of-book indexing. Another standard, proposed by the National Information Standards Organization in 1993, defined guidelines for indexes and related information retrieval devices, also seen as necessary with the advent of computer technology.

The foregoing are minimum requirements for academic preparation and technical information. However, no back-of-book indexer can do a credible job without knowledge of English grammar, index style, and the fundamentals of printing typography and layout. A foundation for back-of-book indexing is also strengthened by work experience in a firm that publishes serious nonfiction books, for example, specialty monographs, textbooks, or reference works.

The factor of training for back-of-book indexing is not so readily disposed of. No set of essential courses (curriculum) has been standardized or even proposed, although such a basic curriculum is fundamental for any body of workers to be recognized as qualified. The idea that anyone can become a successful indexer of books with only the published information available is at best naively optimistic. And yet, a common route to back-of-book indexing, and one widely assumed to be appropriate, is for an author (or author's spouse) to prepare the index, even though either may be untutored and inexperienced. While other routes to indexing (via experience on book or periodical publishing staffs) may be relatively successful, none supports the idea that indexing in general and back-of-book indexing in particular meet the standards for a professional activity.

What has been described and commented upon here are the factors that define the back-of-book indexing process; the process of converting concepts that reveal the substance of an author's thesis in the text into the entry keys to that substance in the index. How well the conversion process is carried out determines how well the purpose of the index is achieved: the unqualified satisfaction of the index user—the "searcher."

It would be easier to consider an indexer's obligation to have been fulfilled with the delivery of an index acceptable to both author and publisher. As important as the delivery contract is, that obligation is secondary to the indexer's obligation to the "searcher"—one that is fulfilled only if the indexer is able to empathize (1) with the author in interpreting his thesis and (2) with the "searcher" in his pursuit of information.

What does it mean when a "searcher" turns to an index to satisfy a need? To the child fact-grubber, the homemaker, the worker in business and the professions, the research scientist, the relentless scholar—to all an index is a tool, one that is unequaled in its simplicity in relation to its utility. There is no clearer testimony to this assertion than its survival and adaptability over centuries as a most effective means of gaining access to all kinds of information. It is impossible to imagine a functioning civilization without some version of the index.

In building empathy with the "searcher," the indexer benefits from exposure to the frustration that every "searcher" experiences with a "bad" index: page numbers that are not precise or properly inclusive; cross-references that are "blind" or elusive in a quarryless chase; concepts indexed as cluster entries with the concept sought buried in an outline of modifications and sub-modifications, not entered as heads as they should be.

The indexer benefits equally from the rewarding experience of satisfying aroused curiosity in a search for an elusive fact or a collection of pieces for solving a research puzzle. Anyone of an inquiring nature knows the mounting excitement in anticipation that *this index* will provide the key for a text with the answer. This identification with the "searcher" more than anything else ensures that the purpose of the index will be realized.

Is there any significance to the indexer's role beyond that of a useful fringe worker in the publishing scene? Is this role unique and how can it be explained? The fact is that in this position "category" the indexer is not alone. Rather, the indexer belongs to an impressive class of specialists who respond to specific intellectual needs—a body including archivists, bibliographers, catalogers (librarians), and even lexicographers.

All these are workers in the domain of records, not just printed works and periodicals, but manuscripts and other kinds of inscriptions—and in the information age, every form of data. All compile keys to information, not the information itself. All share some of the same skills: analyzing, classifying, and organizing keys to information. While the paths that lead to these callings are varied, a common cultural milieu is not hard to find. Curiosity early turns these workers into searchers. They become comfortable with the paraphernalia of learning and acquire an appreciation of solitude. Visualize the material contribution of these workers in the aggregate worldwide, and then imagine their disappearance. A sense of cultural catastrophe is overwhelming.

However, should indexers as a body want something more—status acknowledged by publishers, authors, and fellow synthesizers of information keys alike—a concerted effort by individuals and interested organizations should be initiated. It is not clear whether indexing could, by certification of indexers, achieve this end. This time-honored way has been universally used to separate unqualified workers from those qualified by training and experience. It is also not clear whether publishers, associations of indexers, standards organizations, and academic institutions (e.g., schools of library science) will ultimately recognize the need for such certification and act. If not, the lament of Wheatley nearly a century ago—that untrained indexers do not write good indexes—will continue to resonate.

APPENDIX

1. **Simple line-by-line index for cookbook.** (From Gibson Jefferson McConnaughey. *Two Centuries of Virginia Cooking.* Amelia, Va.: Mid-South Publishing Co., 1977.)

Toast
   French, 152
   fried, 152
   poached eggs on, 150
Toasted pecan pie, 192–193
Toddy, hot apple, 283
Tomato
   catsup, 278
   gelatin (aspic), 84
   pickle
      Clay Hill green, 273–274
      crisp green, 274
   salad, stuffed, 89
   sauce, 145–146
   soup, cream of, 78–79
Tomatoes, 184–186
   baked, 185
   canned, 185–186
   fried, with cream gravy, 184
   preserving of
      green, 38
      ripe, 38
   stewed, 185
Tongue
   cured, 304
   smoked beef, 114–115

2. **Index for political science text showing handling of Arabic names.** (From Rouhellah K. Ramazani, *Iran's Foreign Policy, 1941–1973*. Charlottesville, Va.: University Press of Virginia, 1975.)

Kashani, Mullah, 240, 241
Kashmir dispute, 354
Kavirkhorian oil industry, 36–38, 91, 97, 98
Kavtaradze, Sergey Ivanovich, 96, 98, 99, 101–5, 107, 111, 118
Kazimi, Abolqasim, 78
Kazimi, Baqir, 323
Kellinger, Heinrich, 33
Kennan, George F., 137; on Soviet objectives in Iran, 107, 114
Kennedy, John F.: financial aid and, 320; on foreign aid policy, 360; on land reform, 361
Kermanshah, 30, 32, 38, 205
Khal'atbary, 'Abbas 'Ali, 412, 425; on Iraqi-Soviet relations, 368
Khal'atbary, Arsalan, 283
Khan'ali, 'Abdul Husain, 323
Khanqin, 30
Kharg, 367, 368
Khoramabad, 36, 38
Khorasan, 30, 136, 143, 176
Khorasan oil concession, 98
Khoshtaria concession, 97, 181
Khosrow Khan, 55

3. **Biography index showing management of name homographs.** (From Pamela C. Copeland and Richard K. MacMaster, *The Five George Masons.* Charlottesville, Va.: University Press of Virginia, 1975.)

Mason, Ann Thomson, birth of, 114
Mason, Armistead Thomson, 236
Mason, Beverly Randolph, 264
Mason, Mrs. Beverly Randolph
  (Elizabeth Harrison Nelson), 264
Mason, Catherine, birth of, 21
Mason, Edgar Eilbeck, 242
Mason, Edward, 35
Mason, Mrs. Eleanor Ann C. (wife of
  George Mason VI), 260
Mason, Elizabeth (Mrs. William Roy), 21
Mason, Elizabeth (daughter of George IV),
  100
Mason, Elizabeth (Hooe) (Mrs. George
  Mason V), 238
Mason, Elizabeth Ann Sally, 263
Mason, Emily Virginia, 235, 261
Mason, Francis, 47, 49
Mason, French (son of George II), 21, 46,
  49, 68, 88
Mason, French, Jr., 88
Mason, George, I, 1–18, 20, 26; associates,
  10–11; Bacon's Rebellion and, 15–16;
  birth 1; Giles Brent and, 8, 14; chil-
  dren, 17–18; death and burial, 18; head-
  rights, 9; homesites, 8, 11–12; in House
  of Burgesses, 17; immigration to Virginia, 9; indentured servants and, 12;
  Indian affairs and, 13–15, 17, 18; as
  justice, 12; landholdings, 9, 12, 13, 39;
  litigation, 12; marriages, 17–18; as mili-
  tia officer, 10, 12–13; as officeholder, 9,
  12, 17; patent for land, 10, 12, 13; as
  Royalist, 9; as sheriff, 12; as trader, 12;
  as vestry officer, 13
Mason, Mrs. George, I (Mary French), 15, 17

4. **Index for portfolio on early American culture showing style for works and reproductions.** (From *Winterthur Portfolio II.* Edited by Ian M. G. Quimby. Charlottesville, Va.: University Press of Virginia, 1976.)

Rodney, George Brydges, British admiral, 64, 65, 66
Romanesque revival style, in architecture, 213
Romanesque style, in architecture, 231
Romanticism, youth and, 187–88
Roof, at Tuckahoe, 108, 109, 119
Rosecliff, Newport, Rhode Island, 216
Rosewell: cornice, 108; newel carving, 118; transom, 114; woodcarving, 118
Roslyn, Long Island: Harbor Hill, 213–29; Trinity Church, 229
Ross, Robert, British general, 32, 206n
Rossetti, Dante Gabriel, *The Meeting of Arthur and Guinevere,* 168
Roth, Samuel J., 232
Roumfort, Augustus L., 178n
Rowhampton House, Surrey, England, 131, 132
Rowlandson, Thomas, English caricaturist, 1, 3; style, 29, 31, 32–33; works—*Aerostation Out at Elbows,* 51; *The Connoisseurs,* 31; *High Fun for John Bull,* 29, 31, 32, 49; *The Sculptor,* 31; *Soldiers on a March,* 27, 29, 31, 48; *The Vicar of Wakefield* (Goldsmith) illustration, 33
Royal Academy, 148
Royal Academy of London, 148
Rudolph Ackermann's Respository of Arts, London print shop, 7

5. **Index with numerous proper names, showing the use of lower case for common names.** (From Don H. Kennedy, *Ship Names.* Charlottesville, Va.: University Press of Virginia, 1974.)

Keppel, Augustus, 37
Kipling, Rudyard, 125
Kotebue, Otto, 118

launching ceremonies, 5, 10, 127
laws, 9; English registry, 36, 37, 39, 40;
   Liberian registry, 44; Panamanian reg-
   istry, 44; Rhodian, 29; sea, 29; U.S.
   registry, 37, 40, 41, 42, 43, 113;
   Viking, 32
Lepanto, 30
Liberia, 44
Lichtheim, Miriam, vii
Lind, Jenny, 90
lists, ship. *See* ship registers
Livy, 25
Louis, Saint, 29
Lucian, 25
Luke, Saint, 26
Lyman, John, 110
Lysimachus, 24

6. **Complex scientific index with introductory note.** (From Martin G. Netsky and Samruay Shuangshoti, *Choroid Plexus in Health and Disease.* Charlottesville, Va.: University Press of Virginia, 1975.)

Page numbers in *italics* refer to illustrations; page numbers followed by *t* refer to tables.

Acetazolamide, 103, 126, 142, *144, 145*
  cerebrospinal fluid production and, 142–3, 181–2
Acid phosphatase, *120*–124, *121, 122, 127, 138, 139,* 140, *142*
Actinomycoma, intraventricular, 215
Actinomycosis, 215, 257
Adenocarcinoma, 291
  metastatic, 276–7
  papillary, 270, 271
Adenoma
  acinar (follicular), 274
  nonpapillomatous, 274–5
Adenosine diphosphatase, 135, 138
Adenosine diphosphate, 122
Adenosine monophosphatase, 135
Adenosine triphosphatase, 124, *128, 129,* 135, *136,* 138
Adenosine triphosphate, 122

Amphioxus, 162
Amyloid, 75
Amyloidosis, generalized, 242
Aneurysm, intraventricular, 217, 220
Angioblastic meningioma, 283–4
Angiography, *316,* 327–328
Angioma, 217–20, *218,* 283
Angiostrongyliasis, 259–60
Angiostrongylus cantonensis, 259–60
Antidiuretic hormone, 190
Aqueduct of Sylvius, *12*
Aqueous humor blood barrier, 104
L-Arabinose, 176, *177*
Arachnoid cyst, 203, 272
Area postrema, 15–16, 94
Argentiphilic inclusions, 115
Argyria, generalized, 242–3
Armadillo, 162
Arnold-Chiari malformation, 222

Birds, 5–8, 15
Blepharoplasts, 271
Blood-aqueous humor barrier, 104
Blood-brain barrier, 66
  in brain excretory system, 188
  in chemical environment control, 190
  generalized amyloidosis and, 242
  icterus and, 242
  iron-containing deposits and, 241
Blood cells
  free, 46, 58
  in telencephalic plexus differentiation, 19, 20*t,* *21, 22,* 23, *25* 26, *39*
  ultrastructure, *39,* 46, *55,* 58
Blood-cerebrospinal fluid barrier, 86, 112, 146, 175, 177
  cerebrospinal fluid protein and, 86–7

7. **Cumulative index for Federal government: line-by-line pattern for economics index showing boldface type for identifying volume number (year).** (From *Index to the Manpower Reports of the President, 1963–1972*. Washington, D.C.: US Dept of Labor, Manpower Administration, 1973.)

Year, page

Testing, Informing, Discussion, and Evaluating Program
   (TIDE) ------------------------------- **68**:206–207; **69**:211
Test Program ------------------------------ **68**:199, 200–201
TIDE; see Testing, Informing, Discussion, and Evaluating
   Program
TIMS; see Training in Manpower Services Program
TMRP; see Technology Mobilization and Reemployment
   Program
Tomorrow's Manpower Needs ---------------------- **70**:202
Tool and die maker ----------------------------------- **67**:152
   demand-supply projections ----------------- **63**:108–109
     sources and methodology --------------------- **63**:128
Trade
   employment ------------- **67**:23–24; **68**:178–179; **70**:31;
                            71:15; **72**:35
     projections ------------------ **63**:95–96; **65**:54; **66**:42;
                                    69:66
       1947–62 record ----------------------------------- **63**:21
       1961–68 record ----------------------------------- **69**:32
   part-time (economic) employment ----------- **67**:127, 128
     productivity --------------------------------- **64**:50; **69**:61
     unemployment ------------------------------------ **64**:28, 32
     unemployment rate --------------------------------- **70**:40
     young workers in -------------------------------- **72**:89, 90
Trade Adjustment Assistance Program **71**:44–45, 65, 68

BIBLIOGRAPHY

American Library Association. *ALA Filing Rules*. Chicago: American Library Association, 1980.

American National Standards Institute. *Basic Criteria for Indexes*. New York: ANSI, 1984. (ANSI Z39.5)

American National Standards Institute. *Electronic Manuscripts: Preparation and Markup*, New York: ANSI, 1988. (NISO Z3959)

American National Standards Institute. *Guidelines for Indexes and Related Information Retrieval Devices* (proposal). New York: ANSI, 1993. (ANSI/NISO Z39.4)

Anderson, M. D. *Book Indexing*. Cambridge: Cambridge University Press, 1971.

Austin, Derek, and Dykstra, Mary. *PRECIS*. London: British Library, 1984.

Campey, L. H. Generating and printing indexes by computer. London: ASLIB (ASLIB occasional paper 11), 1972.

Carey, Gordon V. *Making an Index*. 3d ed. Cambridge: Cambridge University Press, 1963.

Chicago Guide to Preparing Electronic Manuscripts. Chicago: University of Chicago Press, 1987.

Chicago Manual of Style. 14th ed. Chicago: University of Chicago Press, 1993.

Cleveland, Donald B., and Cleveland, Ana D. *Introduction to Indexing and Abstracting*. 2d ed. Littleton, CO: Libraries Unlimited, 1990.

Collison, Robert L. *Indexes and Indexing*. 4th rev. ed. London: Ernest Benn, 1962.

157

————. *Indexing Books.* Rev. ed. Tuckahoe, NY: John de Graff, 1967.

Craven, Timothy C. *String Indexing.* Orlando, FL: Academic Press, 1986.

Cutler, Anne G. *Indexing Methods and Theory.* Baltimore: Williams and Wilkins, 1970.

Fetters, Linda. *A Guide to Indexing Software.* Port Aransas, TX: American Society of Indexers. (Issued annually.)

Freelancers on Indexing. Proceedings of American Society of Indexers, San Francisco, 1989. Port Aransas, TX: American Society of Indexers, 1990.

Juhasz, S., and W. Lancaster, J. Knox, and E. A. Ripperger. AKWAS. AMR 32 (December 1979): 1537–1546.

Knight, G. Norman, ed. *Training in Indexing.* Cambridge, MA: M.I.T. Press, 1969.

————. *The Art of Indexing.* London: Allen & Unwin, 1979.

Luhn, H. P. Keyword in context index for technical literature. RG 127, IBM Corp., Yorktown Heights, N.Y., Aug. 1959.

Maddocks, Hugh C. *Generic Markup of Electronic Indexing Manuscript.* Port Aransas, TX: American Society of Indexers, 1988.

Mulvany, Nancy C. *Indexing Books.* Chicago: University of Chicago Press, 1993.

National Information Standards Organization. *Electronic Manuscripts.* Bethesda, MD: NISO, 1988.

Spiker, Sina. *Indexing Your Book.* 2d. ed. Madison: University of Wisconsin Press, 1952.

Wellisch, Hans H. *Indexing from A to Z.* New York: H. W. Wilson Co., 1991.

Wheatley, Henry Benjamin. *How to Make an Index.* London: E. Stock, 1902.

Wheeler, Martha Thorne. *Indexing.* 5th ed. Albany, NY: State University of New York, Albany, 1957.

INDEX

Abbreviations, 96
  alphabetization, 60
  things, 82
Acronyms, 82–83
African personal names, 79
Afterword, 145–149
AKWAS, 140
AKWIC, 140
ALA Filing Rules, viii, 55–56, 146
Aliases, 71–72
Alphabetization
  abbreviations, 60
  decisions for, 57–58
  diacritical marks, 60
  foreign language characters, 61
  humanities text, 84–86
  hyphenated elements, 59
  inversion, 61–64
  letter by letter, viii–xiv, 57–58
  methodology, 56–64
  numbers, 61
  particles, 58–59
  persons, 67–79
  punctuation, 60
  scientific text, 83–84
  social science text, 86–88
  symbols, 60
  technique, 56–64
  time of, 31–32, 57
  word by word, xiii–xiv, 58
Alphabetization and order, 55–88
American National Standard Guide-
     lines for Indexes and Related In-
     formation Retrieval Devices, viii,
     146
American Society of Indexers, viii
Ancient names, 73–74

Appendices, entry copy preparation,
  26
Architecture, 85
Arts, 85–86
Asian personal names, 77
Author index, 5, 53
    See also Names index(es)

Blind cross-reference, 35
Buildings, 63

Capitalization, 90–91
Card indexing, 20–21
Card revision, 109–110
Certification, 148–149
Chinese, 77
Chronology, 65
Compound names, 68–70
Computer-assisted indexing, viii,
    137–144
  advantages, 137–141
  development, 138–141
  electronic manuscript coding, 142–
    143
  for multivolume scholarly edition,
    143
  PC computer compatibility, 142
  revision, 143
  software, 137, 138, 141–142
  specific applications, 140–142
Concepts, 145
  clues, 6–7
  science and technology, 114, 125
  selection, 7
  term categories, 8–9, 11–12
  terminology preferences, 11
Contributor index, 53

Cross-reference(s)
  blind, 35
  definition, xiii–xiv
  editing and styling, 35
  entry copy preparation, 29–30
  external, 49, 50
  faults, x–xi
  format, 49–51
  internal, 30, 49–50
  for multiple indexes, 28
  style, 94–95
  things, 82
  validation, 35, 37

Deadline negotiating, 4–5
Decimal classification system, 97–98
Dedicated indexing program—DIPS, 138, 141
Diacritical marks, 60
Documents, 62–63, 87
Dravidian language names, 78

Editing copy, 32–35
Electronic manuscript. *See* Computer-assisted indexing
El-hi textbooks, 122–124, 126
  "adoption," 123, 126
Encyclopedias, 124, 126–127
Entry construction, 6–17
  format, 47
Epithets, 71–72
Equivalence techniques, 39–41
Et seq., 97
Events, 63, 87

f. ff., 97
Filing. *See* Alphabetization; Order
Finno-Ugric names, 76
First lines, entry copy preparation, 29
First lines index, 53
Foreign language characters, 61
Format, 46–54
  distinctive features, 47–54
  line-by-line pattern, 46, 50–52
  (mixed) modified patterns, 51, 52–53
  order conventions, 48–49

paragraphed pattern, 46, 50–51, 52–53
  scheme variations, 46
Freelance indexing, 128–136
  expenditures, 134–135
  fees computations, 131–132
  financial considerations, 129–130
  "imperfect" proof, 133
  indexer-publisher relations, 130–131
  materials handling, 132–133
  money management, 134–135
  records, 131, 133
  selection of clients, 131
  specialization, 129
  temperament for, 131
  time management, 132–134
  training for, 128–129
  working hours, 134

Galley, indexing from, 39, 40
Geographical names index, 53
German names, 68–69
Germanic languages names, 74–75
Grammar, honoring rules of, 9
Greek names, 76

Head
  capitalization, 90–92
  definition, xiii–xiv
  format, 47–48
  inversion, 62
  parts of speech for, 9
  term categories for, 8–9, 11–12
Homographs, 64
  persons, 67–68
  places, 79–80
  things, 83
Humanities
  alphabetization, 84–86
  concepts identification, 116, 118
  disciplines, 116
  names in, 117, 125
  paragraphed pattern, 118
  perspectives, 118
  works indexing, 117
Hyphenated elements
  alphabetization, 59
  names, 68–70

Illustrations
    entry copy preparation, 26
    page number keys, 64–65
    style, 84
Inclusive numbers, 97
Index(es)
    accuracy and precision, x–xi
    conciseness, xi
    consistency, xi
    definition, ix–xi, xiii–xiv
    faults, x–xi
    history, vii–viii
    items per page, 5
    manuscript length factor, 99–102
    multiple, 53
    multivolume, 41–44
    number of, 5
    text differences, x
    what to omit, 9–10
Index pattern
    line by line, xiii–xiv
    paragraphed, xiii–xiv
Index Society, viii
Indexer(s)
    certification, 148–149
    educational requirements, 146
    identity, 145
    organization, viii
    personality traits, xi–xii
    qualifications, 145–146
    role as information specialist,
        148
    technical knowledge, 146–147
    training, 128–129, 147
Indexer-publisher relations, 2
    negotiations, 130
Indexing
    with cards, 20–21
    from galley, 39, 40
    goals, 1
    prearranged alphabetical guide, 21–
        22
    process, 145–147
    proof for, 19–20
    purpose, 147–148
    to space, 36
    specialty, 112–127
    with strips, 21

    time projection for, 5
    topic, 14–15
Indic languages names, 78
Indonesia names, 78–79
Information gathering, 1–5
    work-projection examples, 3–4
Institutions, 63, 87
Interpersonal factors, 2
Inversion
    alphabetization, 61–64
    definition, xiii–xiv
    format, 48
    personal names, 73
Isolation and recombination process,
        13–14

Japanese, 77–78

Khmer, 77–78
Korean, 77–78
KWIC, 138–140
KWOC, 139, 140

Legal cases, 5, 53, 63, 87–88
    entry copy preparation, 29
    style, 98
Legal text, 121
Letter-by-letter alphabetization, xiii–
        xiv, 57–58
Line-by-line pattern, xiii–xiv, 46
    format, 50–52
    internal cross-reference, 49–50
    punctuation, 91–92, 93
    spacing, 51–52
Literature, 85
Locators
    for illustrations, 64–65
    style, 96–98

Manuscript
    checking, 36–37
    preparation, 36
Materials, 19–20
Medical indexing. See Science and
        technology
Methodology, 1–17
    for alphabetization, 56–64
    information gathering, 1–5

for multiple indexes, 5
for multivolume index, 43–44
"thinking" indexing, 6–17
Mirror entry, 12
Modification(s)
  capitalization, 90–91
  definition, xiii–xiv
  editing and styling, 34–35
  format, 47
  personal names in, 72
Multiple indexes, 53–54
  cross-references for, 28–29
  methodology, 5, 1–44
Multivolume index, 41–44
  materials handling, 41–42
  personnel, 42–43
  technique, 43–44
Multivolume works, style, 97
Music, 85

Names
  African, 79
  alternative, 70–71
  ancient, 73–74
  Asian, 77
  changed, 70–71
  compound, 68–70
  Dravidian, 78
  Finno-Ugric, 76
  Germanic languages, 74–75
  hyphenated, 68–70
  Indic languages, 78
  Indonesia, 78–79
  inversions, 73
  in modifications, 72
  non-English, 73–79
  Romance languages, 75
  Semitic languages, 76–77
  of several parts, 69–70
  Slavic language, 76–77
Names index(es), 53
  entry copy preparation, 27–28
  for science and technology,
    115
Nicknames, 71–72
Notes, 95–96
  entry copy preparation, 26–27
Numbers, alphabetization, 61

Optical character recognition—OCR,
  139
Order, 64–66
  format conventions, 48–49
  for persons, 67–79
Organizations, 63, 87
Outlining, 13–14

Page numbers. *See* Locators
Painting, 85
Paragraphed pattern, xiii–xiv, 46
  format, 50–51
  for humanities, 118
  internal cross-reference, 50
  punctuation, 92–94
Particles, 58–59
Passim, 97
Persons. *See also* specific language
    groups; alternative forms
  alphabetization and order, 67–79
  homographs, 67–68
  inversion, 62
Places, 79–82
  alphabetization, 79–82
  alternative names, 81–82
  changed names, 81–82
  foreign language equivalents, 81–
    82
  homographs, 79–80
  names of several parts, 80–81
Plastic arts, 85
Production, 99–111
  design and estimation, 102–103
  manuscript factor, 99–102
  manuscript length adjustment, 100–
    102, 105
  mark-up for composition, 103–104
  proof, 104
Proof, 19–20, 104
  marking for typist, 22–23
Pseudonyms, 71–72
Publications, 63
Publisher-indexer relations, 2, 130
Punctuation, 91–94
  alphabetization, 60
Reference works. *See* Textbooks and
    reference works
Religion, 121

Revision, 106–111
  with cards, 109–110
  with computer-assisted indexing, 143
  cost factor, 107
  materials, 108
  vs. new index, 108
  planning for, 106–107
  with proof, 110–111
  risk factors, 107
  spot, 108
Romance languages names, 69, 75

Science and technology, 112–116
  alphabetization, 83–84
  concepts, 114, 125
  line-by-line pattern, 115
  references' importance, 114–115
  research report, 113–114, 125
  style, 115
  terminology, 114, 115–116
Scientific research, 113
  publication, 113, 125
Sculpture, 86
Semitic languages names, 76–77
Series, order for, 65
Slavic languages names, 76–77
Social sciences, 119–121, 125–126
  alphabetization, 86–88
  disciplines, 119
  index pattern for, 120–121
  research methods, 119
  "schools," 119, 126
  statistics, 119, 120,
  terminology, 120
  "truth" in, 119, 126
Specialty indexing, 112–127
  for freelance indexing, 129
  humanities, 116–119, 125
  qualifications for, 112
  science and technology, 112–116
  social sciences, 119–121, 125–126
Stage names, 71–72
Strip indexing, 21
Style, 89–98
  capitalization, 90–91
  distinctive treatment, 95–96

page numbers, 96–97
  punctuation, 91–94
  for science and technology, 115
Styling copy, 32–35
Subclasses, order for, 65–66
Submodification definition, xiii–xiv
Symbols, 84, 96
  alphabetization, 60
  capitalization, 91

Table of cases. *See* Legal cases
Tables
  entry copy preparation, 26
  page number keys, 64
  style, 94
Technique, 18–45
  alphabetization, 31–32, 56–64
  alternatives, 20–22
  entry checking, 30–31
  entry copy preparation, 25–29
  entry formulation, 24–25
  entry preparation, 22–30
  equivalence, 39–41
  in-house procedure, 37–39
  manuscript checking, 36–37
  manuscript preparation, 36
  materials, 19–20
  for multivolume index, 43–44
  operations in, 18–19
  with page makeup error, 39–40
  styling, 32–35
  text overview, 24
  for translation, 40
Technology. *See* Science and technology
Text supplements, entry copy preparation, 26–27
Textbook and reference works, 121–124, 126–127
Textbooks
  college, 123
  el-hi textbooks, 122–124, 126
  importance of facts, 122
  sales force, 123, 126
Things
  abbreviations, 82
  acronyms for, 82–83
  alphabetization, 82–88

homographs, 83
preferred vs. alternative cross-
  references, 82
symbols, 84
synonyms for, 82
"Thinking" indexing, 6–17
  isolation and recombination process, 13–14
Titles, 63
  entry copy preparation, 28–29
  inversion, 63
Topic indexing, 14–15
Translation index, 40
Typist, marking proof for, 22–23

Vietnamese, 77–78

WADEX, 140
Wheatley, Henry Benjamin, viii,
  149
Word-by-word alphabetization, xiii–
  xiv, 58
Word index, 53
Word-processor book indexing—
  WPBI, 141
Works
  in humanities, 117
  order for, 66

ABOUT THE AUTHOR

Virginia S. Thatcher attended Wooster College, received a BS in English from Simmons College, and a MSIR (industrial relations) from Loyola University, Chicago. At the Cleveland Clinic Foundation she was supervising editor of medical monographs and contributions to medical journals. She was editor and indexer at the Year Book Medical Publishers; editor-in-chief at Consolidated Book Publishers, Chicago, publisher of encyclopedia reference works and dictionaries; and editor at the University Press of Virginia. She also established editorial procedures at the University Press of New England. While still employed in publishing, she began a freelance editing service for various medical publishers. She also prepared indexes in the humanities and social sciences for several university presses and other agencies including a 10-year index to the *Manpower Report of the President* for the US Department of Labor. She is author of *History of Anesthesia* (Lippincott) and contributions to *Scholarly Publishing*.